SUSTAINABILITY INSIDE-OUT™

GROWTH STRATEGIES FOR CO-PROSPERITY

DILLPREIT KAUR

Author of 'The Action Gap: Business Strategies for Co-Prosperity'

PARTRIDGE

Library of Congress Control Number: 2024922078
ISBN: Softcover   978-1-5437-8278-3
               eBook   978-1-5437-8277-6

Print information available on the last page.

To order additional copies of this book, contact
Toll Free +65 3165 7531 (Singapore)
Toll Free +60 3 3099 4412 (Malaysia)
orders.singapore@partridgepublishing.com

www.partridgepublishing.com/singapore

CONTENTS

ACKNOWLEDGEMENTS

To:

Remembering our ancestors,
yesterday's difficult lessons,
attuning to forgiveness, and
nurturing deep reverence.

Thank you, Mother Earth,
for all that you give us and more.

An Ode

Stay,
don't leave.
Be,
to grieve.

For a time will come,
When all will pass.

A New Earth born,
A New World dawn.

Stay
to see.
Be,
to receive.

~

Poem by Dillpreit Kaur

PREFACE: THE ART OF INTEGRITY

I t is close to midnight, and I am at an empty travellator waiting for my luggage to appear. My impatience is growing, and I am starting to write a complaint letter in my head. I wait a bit longer. I am at Changi airport now. It is unlikely I will face another delay in getting my luggage on this one business trip.

I wait, and anger starts to brew now. I could have paused to breathe. Instead, I marched to the bag reclaim counter to ask where my luggage was and why it had not yet appeared.

> The customer service representative stared at me expressionlessly and answered my question casually: "Did you wait? Sometimes it takes a while."

> In my head, the words repeat: "Did you wait? DID YOU WAIT?! " Now my blood is boiling. I reply with a harsh tone, "Of course I have." Do you know how late it is? This is Changi. Why is there a delay?" My voice tapers off while the representative stares back at me with a blank expression again.

> "Wait at the belt; the luggage will show up."

I am not only dissatisfied but also upset. I have not been taken "seriously." I storm back to the belt.

There, I find my red luggage on the belt.

I grab it and storm out to the taxi stand. "There better be a cab this late; I don't want to turn up at the office sleep-deprived tomorrow," I think to myself.

That was me in 2018. My anger was not due to the job, the customer service rep, or the missing luggage. They were simply the triggers. I was on a spiritual awakening journey that I remained unaware of.

It was a spiritual journey that embodied the ego-death phase. As time passed, I continued to experience my confronting realities to manage my ego. As each experience occurred, emotions surfaced, and deeper pauses were required. Where was this unhappiness coming from, and why am I treating people and myself poorly? What are these expectations, and who am I? I do not want to feel or think this way!

Maybe this resonates with you. Somehow, there is a void in you, even how much you try to fill it with things or achievements. Or, you know you can do better with others. You know something is holding you back from your goals. Or, you are just waiting for a 'safer' option as many opportunities pass you. It is a mind game mostly, coupled with a crippling need to look good, impress or appear a certain way. During this process of awakening, however, we become more aware of how much we deny and hate ourselves by staying addicted to self-inflicted suffering.

This is not anyone's fault. We inherit most of this addiction to suffering through ancestral imprints. We inherit our ego. Fear-based social conditioning builds it up. We adopt unhealthy behaviours and fixed mental models. We think our egos matter. But we are evolutionary beings. We end up missing the signpost as a result, bypassing the exit to continue betraying ourselves. We forget we can hold ourselves. We can face the pain and rebuild better by being aware of our suffering. We forget that after each thunderstorm, there is a rainbow somewhere. We forget there is always a yin to the yang and vice versa. Situations, people and circumstances can always be interpreted from a dualistic lens. Our job is to connect with our higher awareness. It can merge our dualistic realities to create space for both to exist. We must meet ourselves and others with infinite compassion as we proceed. None of us are perfect. There will always be good, and there will always be bad. We can accept it, hold space for our process through it, and get closer to love, light and peace.

Given the complexity of its origins, we avoid meeting this deep, painful desire within us to satisfy ourselves. We prefer staying too busy or distracted to deal with it. This creates a vicious cycle. As we have unresolved pain, we hurt each other until, one day, the universe ends our addiction with an epic crisis. We are shaken and brought to the ground.

We are at the dark night of our soul. It is a soul-led initiation, away from all distractions, including people and places. It puts our humanity at the centre. We begin to grieve for ourselves - how we have neglected and deprived ourselves of safe, loving and supportive experiences. How we have constantly been in harm's way, and why there has been so much suffering when we could fix it. This multi-layered grief and awakening, followed by more grief and maybe some rage, varies from person to person and at what life phase we are at. It is often marked by a desire to hide and not be seen. We grapple with dark emotions that we never knew were there. Depending on our social conditioning, we may judge this process and amplify self-pity, or we recognise a secret magic to alchemise the darker aspects of our human experience to integrate and embody ourselves more. The outcomes of this process depend on what we choose. We may decide to stay in the dark about this, as most of us have, or we may take the courage to transmute and make new of our relationship with ourselves.

Given the dualistic and realist approach to life, most think a good life is such and such. We forget the stoic view of life. It allows space for liminal moments for our grief to emerge. It meets us where we have missed our humanity.

In all of our posturing, we forget that we, too, are vulnerable and incredibly sad inside. We forget that holding space is more than uplifting spirits. It is about allowing others to feel what they need by being there.

As we progress into the dark night of the soul, we learn its ways. We need to surrender into its folds. We must develop trust, faith, and healthier ways of 'being' rather than 'doing'. This can be challenging, especially when we live in a 'what's your 3-year, 5-year, 10-year plan' kind of society.

If we recall the moments of peace we have experienced, perhaps at the top of a hill after a good forest hike, we will stop needing to plan or answer these questions. The universe's plans are better. So, I will show up, present and focus on each moment. I will do what I must to find a happy, fulfilled life. Our intent for peace is all we need for divine love to flow. This healing energy, devotional and divine, can only flow when we let go, believe, and become one with all that is. When we realise that we know nothing, we flow instead of resisting.

Ignoring or neglecting these darker aspects will not make them go away. They will sometimes show up unexpectedly, like a visiting relative from abroad. We might react instead of respond to avoid an unpredictable state of being. So, work through these emotions as they arise. Our shadow side simply needs a trigger - maybe someone said something that is part of our trauma language - and these unaddressed emotions can turn into outbursts. If we stay unaware, we will react instead of respond. We may lash out or sabotage ourselves, especially in environments requiring more professional etiquette.

Watching ourselves in these moments can make us question if we have lost our marbles. Who is this version of me? Why am I acting this way?

All the more, we need to hold space and be compassionate with ourselves. Shame might make us hide. Guilt could consume us as we sink into self-hatred or resentment. We should resolve these challenging emotions in confidence. Trust ourselves. At some point, we must separate to find our true selves. Then, we can return to sync, guided by the will of the whole.

As a highly sensitive empath, I feel everything around me. The upside is that I must sit with these feelings. Are they even mine? Such data mining requires a keen understanding of what is mine, which I struggled with for many reasons. I had to start from scratch. I had to understand what dignity and our humanity are. Why do violations occur? Why do we remain hurt and sometimes hurt others, too? I had to appreciate my inherent emotional intelligence that could pick up double-speak, body language and non-verbal cues.

As a result, I spent much time learning about myself at a deep level. I had to meet all my pain bodies, including my ancestral and karmic ones. I had to learn how to create and enforce boundaries. It is hard if you were raised to be nice or always want to be liked. I had to ask myself why I wanted to be excellent. How does this benefit anyone? I decided to pursue harmony instead because being peaceful is more beneficial than being a nice, complying person. I was enabling unhealthy behaviours and outcomes that were not serving my highest good. Being peaceful evades the need to choose a side and encourages an inward focus instead. We show up, respond and hold space. When necessary, situations end, and we shift out of once uncomfortable situations because our awareness will attract the next best experience for us.

But we usually do not think about the above, much less how we show up and what we do with our time. And we wonder why we have limited faith and belief in ourselves, the universe, and others. This worsens if one believes the world is out to get them or no one can be trusted. These two fundamental beliefs shape our organisational dynamics and societal outcomes today. Co-prosperity is at risk if we stay in victim mode. We must reach out, depend on, and move forward with others. We internalise this victim mode and believe it has to be our truth, but it is not. It only makes us give up on overcoming our limiting beliefs, which are not ours. Sure, it might have started with an experience. Our ruminating mind and the law of attraction reinforced it until it became a belief. Similarly, we can undo it. We can heal ourselves back to a balanced state.

This has been my journey to uncovering transformative leadership. Through these experiences, I have realised we each have a unique path and a proper way of living. Indians call this *dharma*. It is when we choose a code of conduct. It must benefit our hearts, minds, souls, and those around us. It is when we live closest to nature, in reverence for what sustains us. And we help others succeed. When we shift internally, our outer world shifts, too. We do not control or manipulate it.

To hone this self-healing technique, we must heal our thought cycles. Reframing all situations and giving others the benefit of the doubt is our best bet. The moment we believe we know what another person is thinking or feeling, we go down a slippery slope. We end up playing mind games about what was said and not said; disrupting the peace of mind, we are destined for. This becomes easier when we start to develop our heart-brain coherence instead. The mind must visualise what the heart wants. It must not overrule our inner passions with the ego's demands, shaped by the dominant culture. Following our heart also requires unlearning and relearning how to lead with curiosity and openness again. We used to do this effortlessly as children, and somehow, along the way, we shut off our beautiful connection with a world of possibilities, which has caused many of us to become unhappy and succumb to life instead of vice versa.

Unfortunately, self-betrayal becomes a norm when we stay stuck in self-defeating cycles. We allow ourselves to sabotage our happiness and authenticity by believing in negative, self-deprecating thoughts that are primarily unfounded, even if they are karmic or due to ancestral wounds. Our path to our *dharma* has four parts: we must have a clear, intentional purpose, avoid confusion, choose the best path for our growth, not harm others, and seek the best outcome.[1]

As such, we must acknowledge, self-soothe, and change our lives. *Dharma* guides us from within. True affluence emerges from within us as we are renewed by beauty, love, curiosity, discovery, and insights. The universe only 'traps' us in negative cycles if we need to learn specific lessons to realise our potential to grow. Once we are conscious, we can change the patterns. It takes courage and vulnerability in the unknown. Then, we can transform and return to wholeness. This requires balancing our left and right brains to attune to the flow of higher intelligence from our oversoul. We rely more on our left brain for rational, deterministic thinking, and we can benefit from allowing our right brain's intuitive and creative impulses to activate whole-of-mind thinking instead. This will be crucial in escaping our judgmental mindsets and behaviours towards ourselves and others.

Dharma, therefore, is an inbound journey to our true bliss and path. It is a remembrance of what we have arrived on Earth to deliver and share with others so that we may all co-prosper. It is an intuitive journey towards co-existing with all that is. Competition exits the conversation when we are tapped into our unique gifts. Are we showing up to them, honouring and respecting our gifts to prosper in all realms of our lives?

When I chose to drop my ego and learn the difficult lessons, I had to go through many spiritual tests and isolation as I broke down and rebuilt myself, each time a better, kinder and more aligned version of myself. Themes of self-pity and self-contempt emerged as I unravelled

---

[1] D. Chopra, 'Abundance: The Inner Path to Wealth', United States, Harmony Books, 1 March 2022 [audiobook].

these experiences because my unkind, ego-minded version of me lacked self-compassion. It was not until I witnessed and acknowledged the same suffering others go through within me that I could begin meeting myself as a being who needs tenderness and softness.

Because I have gone ahead of your journey, I am here to serve as a loving guide on Earth. We need not fear this process that breaks us down to help us remerge more vital, consolidated, and aligned with our destiny—the intended life path to serve by our abilities and that which can uplift others. We must also be mindful to be grateful for everything, especially the pain. They point out where we have betrayed ourselves, what our needs are, and how we want to be treated instead. The ideal situation is for us to transmute the inherited fear programming to love and appreciate how discovery, healing and recovery have enriched our lives.

Our ancestors had to survive, move to the next best option as soon as possible and do with whatever resources they had. They had to lose as much as gain from moving away from their homelands to 'greener pastures'. They likely did not feel like they belonged for most of their life, or they made every effort to forget their past as if it had never existed. As such, we inherit these glitches and blotches in our psyche regarding our sense of identity, self-esteem and belonging. They likely had to posture and grow their egos to overcompensate for the insecurities of their time, mainly as defence mechanisms. They likely made decisions that perpetuate deception, betrayal or sadness, which just gets left to weaken family lines until a new ancestor, such as us, takes up the mantle to heal this once and for all. To complete our families by bringing back hidden and forgotten stories to the fore. To restore balance in thoughts and deeds for prosperity to be a reality. We must forgive our ancestors who did not make the best decisions and choose to do better now.

Therefore, a complete death of our old self becomes integral in this process. This is so we can allow our soul to come back online more and more in our day-to-day decision-making and manifest our destiny. This will require a stronger focus on our heart-mind, heart-gut and heart-womb coherences. **Heart-mind:** what are we thinking and projecting that nourishes us and supports the growth of others? **Heart-gut:** what are we doing to feel safe and create more safety for others? **Heart-womb/**

throat: what are we birthing/creating in this world – how will it serve our humanity and that of others?

Authentic communication emerges when we remove the emotional charge from words that previously triggered us and widen our vocabulary for happy thoughts and exchanges.

The last decade alone (2014-2024) has been evolutionary for us here in Singapore and the world, with the number of transits we have seen and experiences we have had and continue to have. The COVID-19 pandemic did not bring on just one new normal, but it continues to show us its ripple effects, as one ripple causes another shift. Everything else shifts whenever we shift our mindset, take a stand, or commit to an action. Our anxiety levels only skyrocket when we are unaware of this. This is why consciousness work is crucial and highly beneficial to help us heal our anxiety about the unexpected. The more we sink into this new way of being with change, the more we can open up to the evolutionary possibilities available.

What if we could start this journey earlier?

Ambition does not have to come at the cost of our health and well-being. Its origins should caution us against making it our primary goal. The phrase 'a striving for a favour' reflects our historical roots in feudalistic societies. Although we have moved to constitutional systems, we still feel a lingering sense of subservience to an imaginary authority. This leads us to let unhealthy power dynamics shape our self-worth and identity. Misguided leadership has kept different social classes trapped in outdated ways of thinking, helping to maintain the elitism of the past—and, in some cases, the present. When we recognise these underlying dynamics that influence our environments, we gain the freedom to create rather than produce (see Table 1).

Create	Produce
• Value adding	• Imitating
• Innovative	• Status quo
• Brand enhancing	• Quality control
• Meets future/unexpected needs	• Demand based
• Fresh	• Business continuity

Table 1: Differences between creating and producing outputs

We need to go inward to reconnect with the lost islands of our soul and reclaim our very power to manifest our *dharma*. Please note this is different from wishing for a specific life, etc. It has to be aligned with our current reality, what we have experienced and what we can tangibly do right now to move forward. No drastic action is required, and instant manifestation is possible when we show up in each moment, present-minded and focused on what will serve the highest good for ourselves and those around us. Our *dharmas* aim to show us our unique path to happiness, which will look different for each of us. When we strive for similar things, we soon realise it is futile when we still feel a void. Our *dharma* is the only path that can offer us fulfilment from overcoming the lessons we need to achieve our highest potential in being of service to others.

So, when and how can we achieve this alignment with our *dharma*?

When we quit betraying ourselves, we become receptive, which includes receiving from others. Self-sovereignty from a receptive state ensures we are non-judging, aware, and detached. We can recognise our self-denial and help move ourselves into ease. We can differentiate fear of the new/unknown from our intuition or inner guidance forewarning us. At this point, we are aligning within. We begin living as intended, seeing past the veils or illusions before us and walking into our freedom.

We step into an ancient knowing that we co-prosper when we give and receive in balance. We build to restore and revitalise communities. We bring everyone along, and we all thrive. There is no separation or difference that we cannot heal. How, then, do we awaken that already innate in us – our propensity to love ourselves and others in unfathomable ways? What would bring us the peace of God found in each sunrise but lost in every tension? What is it that drives us to our wounds, dilemmas and our joy? The deep, kind, stable, non-achievement-based essence of our true being state?

Heart consciousness is knowing we are all gifted uniquely and accepting life in its multifaceted glory. Like nature, we are neither predictable nor meant to be. We are cyclical and seasonal—we can rest when we need to, ideate when we need to, create when we need to, and harvest when we need to. Reevaluating how we have been living our lives and, more importantly, what ends it has helped us all achieve matters.

If we look at outcomes towards nature-positive societies, carbon abatement is not the only and sole way forward. Equally important is water and waste management. We cannot afford to be myopic based on the levels of awareness we allow ourselves to access—either out of convenience, complacency, or compliance. Nature always knows better; we have to look to her for answers.

Accurate outcomes can only emerge when we address the inequalities within ourselves and our communities. This healing process starts with recognising self-betrayal, often from internalised beliefs devaluing our worth. Additionally, many families carry generational burdens of unresolved grief and trauma, which can distort relationships and perpetuate cycles of dysfunction. Similarly, inequities arise in organisations from ineffective conflict resolution practices and unequal compensation, leading to a culture of mistrust and disengagement. On a societal level, discriminatory policies and a lack of truth and reconciliation regarding historical injustices further entrench inequalities as well. We cannot hope to create fair and just outcomes without acknowledging and addressing these systemic issues. Healing requires a concerted effort to confront and rectify these deep-rooted disparities across all levels of our lives. It requires radical self-honesty and compassion to overcome the perceived hurdles of change.

We are all mirrors to one another.

Embodying a regular practice to contemplate is vital for our human existence, especially with so much happening around us. Where am I stuck? How can I emerge more gracefully? What do I not like about a situation or person? Work from there to reconcile ourselves to wholeness because every moment is a lesson with a blessing. At the same time, boundaries are of utmost importance. We can all learn to communicate what we need, and if the other individual cannot meet us there, part amicably. Let us welcome the insights they offer us so that we may evolve by addressing our physical pain, emotional patterns and mental frames towards a healthier, zero-still-point level of consciousness where these extremes and nuances do not matter. Let us take responsibility for our healing.

When we do this purification work, we wipe our mirror squeaky clean. Through us, crystalline clarity emerges to help others see a bit clearer. We become lighthouses, and previous tense experiences begin to drop away. We soften and can see things as they are now. We overcome powerlessness. We become compassionate.

This is when we begin to have capacity to *think* about what it means to be genuinely sustainable.

For me, it is when we unite rather than divide, harmonise rather than demonise and ensure rather than assure. This is co-prosperity, in short. We are dignity conscious – providing equal recognition to everyone to cease striving for power - and we are rebuilding better, with each other in mind. It needs our unparalleled regard for the Divine within each one of us so that we can unleash tremendous creativity that will bring forth the innovation we need for a green, safer and kinder future.

Only integrity can heal the many ways we betray ourselves, especially self-honesty. If we genuinely want sustainable change, it is happening. The question is almost always whether we follow through on what we say we wish to do. This is where compassion will be required—self-compassion and compassion for others. We can only do what we are aware of. Most of the time, we are unaware of how to move forward, move past rhetoric and substantively move the needle. We have internalised scripts of how we need to be, act and say, when in reality, it may not be 100% us or what we wish to embody. We may know better and feel stuck for some reason to pander to an outdated belief system or old-world thinking. I plead with you to make the shift yourself and influence your environment to reframe it so the system can self-heal.

New World[2] thinking will not disrupt and remove safety from the status quo. It will help us stay compassionate during the transits and ensure we are constantly recreating with safety in mind: safety of mind, body and soul. With dignity consciousness, we respect perceived differences, include ourselves and others organically, and progress further together. This helps us co-prosper knowing that diversity is necessary. It is acceptance and individuation that are better as a whole. Looking at thriving forests, it is the complex ecosystem from the cross-pollinating and mutative effects of species interacting with one another that the whole system thrives. To recreate it via reforestation is almost challenging as we humans have forgotten the ways of nature and that it restores in random occurrences, sporadic growth and at different timelines. Our linear timescales, simplistic targets and single materiality plans are only suitable for the short term. To create co-prosperous outcomes, we must surrender our selfish agendas and plug into the whole. We might even have to suspend our desired outcomes and allow organic movements and shifts to occur, much like the natural world.

History has shown our difficulty with such self-sovereignty as protectionist and territorial agendas ruined empires and ripped apart communities that once celebrated organic growth and mutual reciprocity. We are all meant to show up as ourselves and work towards aligning with a beneficial vision based on our current state. Heaven is precisely where we are, and if we can commit to that, soon, the world will be thriving not just in pockets of Eden but in bustling cities and forgotten lands. Knowledge, as we know, is ever-growing, and the goalposts will keep shifting. If we can build ourselves up with emotional resilience and intellectual persistence,

---

[2]   *This book will use the phrases 'New World' and 'New Earth' interchangeably, where relevant. Content related to the 'New World' will discuss future-focused innovative strategies, leadership, and business paradigms. In contrast, content related to the 'New Earth' will address environmental consciousness and holistic well-being, emphasising sustainability, interconnectedness, and a more profound respect for nature.*

we become unshakable: come what may, we can overcome any situation. This begins with us being conscious of our dignity and that of others through the diverse identities we represent and their intersectionality. We all have solutions, and any problem can be overcome together. This coming together will require a dispersion of our ego-minds, ego-identity and social constructs.

Harmony is within reach if we *allow* it and do *not* resist it.

And that will need to be the basis for Industry 5.0. One where we are focused on facing challenges to grow into our most evolved selves with technology has a catalyst. This mindset nevertheless requires a daily practice of self-awareness, self-love and self-care. Something many of us misunderstand, take for granted or ignore. This has been and continues to be the only truth that can set us free and unleash our creativity by unlocking our intuition.

The perennial question has been and remains – are we ready to meet our *infinite* selves?

This book offers ways for us to begin healing and dissolve the fissures as new ancestors and leaders of our families and organisations. Many have awakened to this possibility within and around them; it is only time that we join them and rebuild better each time we are challenged.

You know what it is like to heal deep-seated pain with band-aid solutions; it is still there, it still grows, and it prolongs our inevitable recovery. Sustainability Inside-Out™ aims to bring us through a self-discovery of much-needed New World leadership. What we invest in today matters for the future we are building. Where our attention goes, our energy flows. I hope you will journey with me through this book to become a champion for a co-prosperous world where we prioritise balance, well-being, sustenance, ethical conduct and spiritual evolution in how we think, act and be. It begins with believing that we are cosmic beings here on Earth to have a human experience and heal. In each of our families is an awakened seed; if you are reading this, it is likely you. Let's courageously answer the call to heal ourselves, our families and communities. Let's co-prosper together.

INTRODUCTION:
THE SCIENCE OF REJUVENATION

'Rejuvenation' is to see things with fresh eyes, to make anew, and to be in awe of life. This is the synergistic nature of Mother Earth and its co-creative potential for us to work alongside her. From deep sea to asteroid mining, our race to secure commodities for our advancements in technology and defence is astounding. As long as we have a business case with a short-term return on investment, we will keep extracting resources instead of considering circularity in how we take, make and dispose of existing resources in our procurement, production and consumption loops.

We are equally members of a galaxy as we are of a planet. Our responsibility for care lies beyond what is seen, known and heard. It is also time we notice that we are living within Gaia, a living, breathing planet on its own. We are beings within her who have the potential to seed harmony or continue with our discord mentality. I know this because I have witnessed how we can tear each other apart as much as we can connect. We are embedded in thinking we are separate from each other, but we are not. This new programming can lead to much-needed quantum shifts towards our spiritual growth. It can usher in miracles of unconditional loving thoughts, emotions and behavioural patterns we never thought possible before. We each have come on Earth to seek and embody this potential.

Indeed, we are in the age of tremendous transformation. It is time for us all to return to nature: both Mother Earth and our true soul nature. We are loving beings, kind beings and happy beings. If this does not resonate, please note where the dissonance regarding your beliefs is coming from. When we do not believe, we succumb to our 'rational' mind instead. We allow ourselves to conjure many scenarios and possibilities at one go, often at the expense of our heart essence. This is how our ego rules the mind, which tends to put others or ourselves down because we lose touch with our humanity. We forget that being human is difficult, and we each have baggage to sort out.

I would like us to imagine ourselves within the womb of Mother Earth, where she is holding us. Can we feel the rush of pure spring water from her ever-flowing waterfall? Can we notice the tinges of colour as birds take flight around us? What sounds do we hear that surpass the usual humdrum of cityscape noise? What images can we picture in our minds? How do we feel when we are indeed one with her? We can bridge this disconnect by bringing this sense of tranquillity and peace into every environment we are in. It requires us to be fully embodied here on Earth. When we are here right now, we can take good care of ourselves and our environment.

This book calls for focusing on spiritual evolution via a co-prosperity lens. It will allow us to unpack the real needs of our people, economic systems and Mother Earth with circular economic approaches in mind.

Nothing is within our control except our spiritual evolution based on the choices, words, and thoughts we project outward. No one has a hold on us as we think, and going against a grain of thought or social conditioning is the very essence of nature. We are meant to be unique embodiments of what makes a diverse, rich ecosystem. We think we are happy when we get something, be someone or achieve something when we have always had the propensity to be happy regardless of external circumstances. Our happiness lies in how we see this world and how it happens. We are happy when we can empathise with the struggles of others, not to interfere but to hold space and lead with compassion. Through these actions, we inevitably project our divine cosmic self, this unshakeable essence of pure love and light.

With synthesised content from my pursuit of Truth and real-world exposure during my travels meeting other seekers, the book offers step-by-step guidance for us to heal ourselves and become responsible dwellers within our cosmos – each empowered to make the quantum leaps we need to usher in New World thinking and leadership that will support a broader view of alternative business development opportunities than we have currently. Such a lens will also allow us to see that spiritual evolution calls for determined action towards our self-realisation on Earth, primarily to experience freedom. We discuss this further in the chapters ahead.

'The Action Gap: Business Strategies for Co-Prosperity' discussed the Limits to Growth report, which we rehash here to remind ourselves that there is a limit to how we grow and want to grow.

a) To what end?
b) With what means?
c) At what cost?

We are *not separate* from the whole.

This is where the story of our genesis will be pertinent. We come from a family line, whether known or not. We develop our consciousness from experience and are more interconnected than we think. It is time we move past this ignorance.

There is always an argument for and against situations. The good news is that the more conscious we are in how we think and operate about these challenging dilemmas, which are often moralistic, the better we can make decisions about them.

It is no longer acceptable to accept less than mediocre because someone cannot meet us where we are or is limited in their ways to respond adequately. Instead, we need to negotiate how to meet each other where we are and encourage both parties to grow and keep growing for the better.

Many of us guard old hegemonic rule systems over others, whether in the private or public sectors, and this needs to be addressed here. The New World social contract calls for reasonable compensation for historical inequities that still perpetuate in our times, even in subtle ways. As gatekeepers of the present world systems, let the reforms begin.

The actions of one state government do impact others elsewhere, even if there is no seemingly direct link to the situation. For example, the Internet curfews of July 2024 in Dhaka impacted me in Singapore as I could not connect with a friend even though I am not Bangladeshi nor related to this person. I need not care per se, but it does affect me. In an age of hyper-connectivity, we often take our freedom to call, Zoom, and Facetime for granted. These minute disruptions compound over time, leaving tears and scars in our collective psyche that we all inherit whether we know it or not. These bound us in return, and we must overcome these fissures on Earth before we may genuinely ascend. But how?

Quick fixes are no longer the solution; taking responsibility for *rejuvenation* is.

Our backstories will be crucial in helping us shapeshift into the embodied humans we have yet to be. For most of us, owning and respecting where we come from, what we experienced, and how we overcame each setback will be the priority healing balm.

At this point, we can see, hear, and hold space for ourselves at every moment of our past trajectories to assure our younger selves that we feel deeply for their pain and no longer need to hold on to this story. Things are and can be different now. By reconciling the lost fragments of our esteem, hopes, and dreams, we can weave a present-minded consciousness so steeped in the heroism of our suffering and recovery that we become formidable in our resolve to make changes towards more care, love and light in our lives.

This will not be easy as most of us practice false consciousness to cope with the sordid or complicated parts of our history, including the stories we hear of ancestors and their journeys. What we receive are mere fragments of the whole story, and we must heal much more than that. The collective has endured much grief, suffering and pain with regards to being abandoned at some point in our timelines, being rejected by another, rejecting another, superseding our status over another, being oppressed by others, as well as dark wounds of hatred – both self-inflicted and imposed.

We will each have to sit to awaken our inner light. This will surface as suffering and pain. Our job is to identify, accept, and, like a surgeon, diagnose, extract and seal up open wounds to allow ourselves to recover our true identities as innocent, young, and fresh-eyed children again. There is no end to our potential; we need not hold ourselves back anymore.

Those aware of our true origin as souls beyond this physical form know this to be inherently true. We are part of a whole that needs healing, and when we rise to the challenge of dealing with the hurt, the trauma, and the pain, we inevitably heal others, especially those around us. This magic, synchronicity, and transformation available now cannot be understated.

Integrity will be vital as we proceed forward.

How do we show up, honestly address our hurts and frustrations with others, and reconcile to get much closer to ourselves? How do we bring down the barriers we have put up around our hearts, our bodies, and our minds?

So many of us live with baggage from past experiences that no longer serve us despite their burdens. We accept this baggage for many reasons and get comfortable with it because we fear the unknown. When unresolved, we pass it on to our children, who unknowingly carry on this legacy of pain. We must, however, awaken to these tensions and stressors and restore our inner harmony so that our families and personal lives can start thriving holistically from a deep space of union with all around us. These effects will be profound globally. Imagine if we all took responsibility and started healing in our respective corners of the world. The trajectories informing our unsustainable future and growth addiction could be overcome.

Are we willing to return to nature, our true nature and close the action gap? Are we willing to see each other as ourselves? Are we willing to work together as one?

Looking at our financial systems and governance networks, a progressive movement is emerging that is trying to understand the complexity of this issue, albeit from a compliance/risk mitigation standpoint. We are still mainly in defence mode and thinking about preserving or protecting what we believe is ours. This protectionist frame of thinking is further challenged by territorialism – this notion that we have the right to exercise our sovereignty however we like. We have seen this with the decline of democracy from illiberal actors. Globally, we perpetuate these cyclical imbalances in our governance systems by fuelling the negative Media coverage, which most bad actors appreciate. Our international aid and rights-based campaign further expands energy, calling to restore 'justice' when we know sovereignty means each country has the right to govern as it wishes. Our values as more democratic or liberal citizens are commendable, and when we go inward instead, tune into the collective energy and send healing light – peace is more likely than this romanticised 'righting of a wrong' we seek. Through this process, we gain wisdom to rejuvenate our essence towards present-life conscious creation instead of what may have transpired in our past lives.

The thing is, we can all resonate with wars and the injustices of our time because somewhere deep down in our psyche, we or our family line have directly experienced this loss. At some point, we have been in the same situation.

We are re-experiencing this to remember and reconnect with our lost humanity if we have been over-extending ourselves, which plenty of human rights workers and caregivers do. And if we feel nothing or numb, it reminds us to forgive ourselves, for we may have been perpetrators of such crimes and not known better. The roles we took on and are taking are not personal. They are part of a great divine play to bring us all back to balance, and the less we resent or rationalise it, the quicker we can step into happiness specially curated for us based on the exact experiences we have gone through and need to, to appreciate the splendour when it comes. The attitude of gratitude will be our best antidote as we all transfigure and grieve the loss of versions of ourselves we once knew and perhaps spent a lot of time and money curating. Now, we may step into a more aligned version suited for the cosmic duty we signed up for on Earth: to create rose gardens everywhere we go.

As a descendant of an immigrant family and woman of colour, I unknowingly knowingly entered the workforce with many inherited notions of the 'injustices' my family and generations before me have faced. Naturally, as a first-generation university graduate, the passion and strife to stand up for what is 'right' was strong. I pursued my Masters in Human Rights and Democratisation, internalising liberal democratic values my Western education offered me only to see its application in my home region – Asia Pacific – having their challenges.

I then began my journey from a place of 'perhaps there is lack of knowledge or capacity-building' only to realise that there is a socio-cultural and historical context to governance and social contracts that are often whitewashed in pursuing standardised ideals of modern-day governance. To no fault of these international standards, given they, too, emerged from fraught historical journeys that included much war and devastation. A common, unifying form of governance in the form of representative democracy, therefore, seems a reasonable answer to restoring peace and cooperation. However, it becomes more challenging to implement if we disregard the unique cultural beliefs and traditions of respective communities and how they communicate to make meaning today.

This tension in my education and real-world politics brought me towards Buddhist teachings several times. Each time I pursued understanding my nature through meditation, I would envy the detachment with which the monks and nuns I interacted with had towards the 'outside world'. They knew what was happening, some better informed than me, yet unperturbed. This is where I understood our energy is better utilised going inward to develop such a rich sense of self and inner knowing that we do not contribute more 'noise' to our environments and systems. When we engage with chaos, we become it. Learning to step back, see the bigger picture and hold space, especially for ourselves, serves a far greater outcome. This is why we must reflect on our best intentions and recalibrate a new way of being.

This begins with knowing what calms our nervous systems down.

Are you ready? Tick any of the boxes/activities below that help you connect better within:

- ☐ Journalling
- ☐ Breathwork
- ☐ Movement / Exercises
- ☐ Yoga Nidra
- ☐ Power naps
- ☐ Meditation
- ☐ Being in Nature (including Water)
- ☐ Being yourself
- ☐ Not worrying or overthinking
- ☐ Receiving kind words of encouragement
- ☐ Receiving love and attention from others
- ☐ Ensuring all needs are met
- ☐ Knowing you are on your path (via signs, symbols)
- ☐ Knowing you are connected (via prayer, blessings)
- ☐ Knowing there is a solution to every problem

While we may have forgotten our co-creative abilities and commitment to our *dharma* to bring back balance in our lives and on this Earth, there is still time. We have time if we take the first step towards restoration now. Suppose we start caring—caring for ourselves, others, and Mother Earth. If we block out the noise, fear-mongering, and outright violations and breaches occurring now, we can feel safer and kinder to each other. We can overcome this, and we have done it before.

We are nature. Our bodies are made of water, air, matter and fire. We can co-create synergistically with the resources from Mother Earth and her beings. Our current outputs contain elements that can contribute to producing biofuels through advanced waste management, for example. We live on a water planet, with 70% of Earth and human bodies being water. We can thrive by respecting and embodying the spirit and intelligence of water. We ensure we are transparent and clear, like its essence, and flexible and smooth, like its flow. The moment we are stuck in life, we are stuck somewhere in our bodies. Our energy cannot close its loop, and unaddressed pain causes our energy to stagnate. We can undo this with the healing power of water. Whatever happens to water, it always returns to its pure, indestructible state. We can embody this quality as well.

We can respect our healing journeys, remove the self-judgements, ensure self-love and self-compassion and move past self-denial and self-betrayal.

We can heal this pain, unblock the passage, and help the waters in our system flow again so that we can move forward. The key to this is balance, finding the middle ground in everything we do and being content with what is and around us. We know we can embody this with gratitude every moment and for everything we receive—even the negative, for it has a lesson. As conscious beings, we will honour integrity to uphold this balance. This will come with profound reverence for the sacred in our lives, such as access to clean water.

Water runs the planet, from the rains to the groundwater to the oceans, and it sustains all life through drinkable and accessible water. None of us can do without it, and neither can the planet. As a transient elemental energy, water's ability to return to its natural state of purity reflects our ability to restore ourselves despite our environments. Water is pure in its most genuine essence, and so are we.

This book calls for a balance that would strengthen harmony and open ourselves to innovation beyond what we thought possible, bringing new possibilities that enrich the whole and protect other ecosystems in space and underwater. We must let go of our egoic notions of self and merge into one consciousness. When we see ourselves as water and how we are one with the waters of this planet, we can see how we flow through every ecosystem and are, therefore, interconnected.

We must respect everything that sustains us – clean air, nourishing soil, mineral-rich water and enriching fire. We need to let go of our defences, including our dependencies. It only disconnects us from what sustains us. We must pivot to energy-positive business models and learn from communities still connected to Mother Earth, only taking what they need. Our systems must be like nature – self-learning, adaptive and flexible instead of rigid and rules-based. This will help us to survive climate change and its associated public health and infrastructure-related disruptions.

Overall, we must redefine what wealth means to each of us. Have we allowed a tool (in this case, money) to be used on this planet to bind us to the notion of being and existing as a cohesive entity at the planet's expense instead?

In his documentary, *The Human Element*, Mattew Testa shares the story of a mining company that invested in building a renewable energy plant to create jobs for the community impacted by the closure of its mines. This need not be the story of one company; it can be the story of all companies. Our business continuity plans can factor in co-prosperity to restore trust and rebuild societies in alignment with higher values.

Co-prosperity is, therefore, a call for values-based management. It is EGSEE[3] -

*How do we **economise** value creation beyond profit generation and shareholder dividends to more livelihood and job creation to support communities that lack access to the means to do so?*

*Are we **governing** our processes to ensure the challenges of our times are not seen as threats but opportunities for regrowth?*

---

[3]   *More details in D. Kaur, 'The Action Gap: Business Strategies for Co-Prosperity', 2024, Partridge.*

*Can we **socialise** our thinking to encapsulate sustainability inside out, making workplaces safer and healthier psychologically and ensuring the knowledge-skills gap is closed by working hand-in-hand with institutions of higher learning to co-create more aligned business objectives for the broader economy?*

*Do we conduct ourselves as **ethical** decision-makers and workers in an organisation with self-integrity and transparent communication with one another?*

May we **coexist** with responsible and productive action towards the **environments** in which we operate as businesses and individuals by taking empowered action to ensure the outcomes we communicate truly respect the resources we procure, utilise, and deliver as our products and services. These pivots can take place gradually and not at the expense of our comfort zones. It requires a commitment to understanding how - based on comprehensive due diligence, gathering intelligence, exercising gratitude for what has worked, and nurturing what needs to happen for tangible yields to come through.[4]

We must consider all available scales of information and technological platforms to harmonise our efforts in providing invaluable information on the granular to macro impacts on our agricultural systems, supply chain and logistics transportation flows, urban city planning, public transportation and mobility networks, building and construction limits, as well as physical and transitional risks on extreme weather patterns via our disaster and emergency response readiness programmes. This interoperable system needs to be accessible to all, with a socially binding clause to contribute transparent, real-time information that could save more lives

---

[4]   *Please refer to our dignity® approach on how to implement a viable EGSEE approach for your organisation at www.goalweaver.biz.*

and curb infrastructure losses, especially in climate—and economically vulnerable regions.

Private actors must come on board to safeguard their long-term investments and valuations. We need less reliance on intergovernmental bloated systems like the United Nations and encourage leaner, streamlined operatives who can mobilise quicker at localised outposts. We also need our governments to fear less economic recession and take reasonable action to communicate clear nature-positive roadmaps even if there are trade-offs with established businesses that are unsustainable in their operations. For corporations, adopting double materiality as a core metric in sustainability evaluation is how we may make amends should we wish to move past taking Mother Earth for granted.

We will create new value by building integrated water, heat, and nutrient recovery systems. Like most industries, we must de-risk and improve operational efficiency with real-time data monitoring, prognostic analysis, and good data governance. We all know this is where the challenge lies: competition.

In the New World, competition transforms into collaboration because we each have a competitive edge that complements the other, even if it is the same product or service. We might have a proprietary approach or automation and can work together to create new value. We move past price wars as a definition of business viability and consider what would move the needle for us as a society. We operate like networked bees, and we bring everyone forward. We leave no one behind. This will require robust spiritual evolution to embody this mindset, way of living and embodied knowing of harmonic resonance. We are interdependent beings, and each deserves support as we atone and attune to what is needed for New Earth consciousness.

No one has the crystal ball. While this book offers some semblance for framing the issue, addressing it with actionable insight and ascertaining its impact will be difficult but not impossible. This is where educating ourselves on circular business models will be useful. It offers a systems thinking and green value cycle approach to business product development, which may open up new markets and business opportunities for established players. The global climate challenge is the perfect classroom for us to learn this. We are at nature's mercy as rising temperatures, raging wildfires, and devastating floods cause infrastructure and ecosystem services to be lost. We know how vulnerable we are as our timelines for course-correcting shrink and our resources become increasingly challenged. Due to our capitalistic lens of value creation, we are still plagued by short-term thinking despite efforts by industry coalition bodies to develop net-zero transition plans for the near, medium and long term.

The increasing call to consider nature's ecological impact means our economic and industrial pursuits must adapt to become purpose-fit for upcoming nature-positive societies. Whether we like it or not, this will happen. Therefore, this calls for reconciling what we have been cut off from all this time in our psyche and behaviour.

We are nature, so adaptation is an innate ability of ours. We can safely trust that we have the in-built survival mechanisms to survive any storm. Spiritual evolution ensures we see ourselves honestly and grow into the aspired leaders who do our best to mitigate our footprints concurrently with more macro developmental plans. We will have to change a common misconception that sustainability is only related to climate change when it is everything. We will need to think beyond carbon to include our well-being, water and waste management as well. As we know, sustainability is the practice of ensuring we have enough resources for future generations. These mindset shifts can only occur when we are tuned within. In this world, obstacles are signposts for clarity and ease. If intense emotions emerge from obstacles, they affirm how much we wish to proceed with this task and clarify why we aim for this goal. Validated, we can determine how we view the situation differently, what variables are mutable, and how we may meander around the obstacle without feeling defeated or discouraged. We pick ourselves up again, and we can keep going. This is the New World thinking and spirit.

When we go at anything with sheer force or from one angle, as we have witnessed historically, we may realise that we accumulate more backlash or deadlock instead. This is undesirable; instead of seeing the situation as it is, we may use further distractions to cover it up. We inevitably invest more willpower to amplify the unwanted outcomes when we can accept and course-correct at any time. We need to transcend this line of thinking: that we can break through one day with sufficient force. It must leave our belief systems, cultures and ways of being with each other. It comes at a heavy cost. On the other hand, when we facilitate new ways of being creative and honouring our gifts, passions, and strengths, we allow situations and the other to be. We let go of forced persistence or resistance and attract more suitable outcomes.

Obstacles are, therefore, a means to rethink and adapt. We need not raise our defences, back away, or give up. We have to flow and flow towards them so that we may see how to get around them. With spiritual evolution as our focus, we zoom into the respective fear-based programming to undo the patterns of our words, actions, and thoughts to excel in what truly calls out to our inner passions and drive. Most of us might fall into the obstacle of surfing backwards and dry up from not trying. We may even imagine the obstacle as though it is not there and consider the backward momentum of our surfs as movement as well – a double whammy situation. We may also form a lagoon right before the obstacle to wait and see if anyone comes through to get around the obstacle. We are clever this way, but to our detriment, a lagoon soon stagnates and starts to evaporate if untended. *We must always regain our essence and be brave enough to keep moving.*

Our self-preserving habits of maintaining the status quo, avoiding challenges, and not taking risks to address problems that present a need to evolve have to change. We can do this without restrictions and labels to accept how life opens up. This requires deep surrender and suspension of the largely imbalanced masculine[5] ways of being in our current reality.

What if I told you your origin? My dear reader, you are infinite light, love, and joy. We chose to be here right now. We can choose to heal,

---

[5]   *Do something, be someone, produce anything so that others can see how we manifest our ideas into form. How we show up in this defined world needs to be fixed so that we can be reliable and dependable for others to lean on. Issue emerges when we*

overcome the lies about our true nature, and grow in our abilities to see things as they are and what they can be. The need of the hour now is for us to let go of everything we once knew. We must unlearn and relearn to return to our natural state, no matter what transpired, right up to this point of reading this sentence.

This book has been written with the intention for all of us to return to ourselves, grow roots wherever we are, and ensure they are supportive for future generations to thrive. A significant component would be healing, healing all the fissures and unknown dark recesses of our being so that we leave behind gardens for future generations. We are taking the next step to realise our life's purpose and will do it responsibly with all who are connected with us. We will aim to hold space for each other and grow our compassion muscle so that we are no longer bothered by the pesky emotions and feelings that once kept us captive in negative thinking loops.

Everyone truly has the best intentions for each other based on their level of awareness and experiences. Seeing one another at a soul level will remind us of this fact each time we feel injustice or fear bubbling up within us. Even those with murderous instincts are victims of a poor choice made at some point in their ancestral history to repeat the narrative until this pain of being separate from another is healed. We are infinite and have always been embraced by infinity. Recognising our quantum nature is where we will truly evolve into whole, complete and healed humans. The soul has always been one with the Source, so the more we connect back to within ourselves, the more we connect with our true essence and sense of freedom.

This is held at the individual, family, and organisational levels. Everything is relational, including how we perceive and act and see things. The sooner we let go of old patterns and unhelpful habits and gravitate towards accepting and loving ourselves as we deserve to be loved by others, we unlock new paradigm shifts for ourselves. Ego-deaths will be integral to this process. Like an onion, we will be peeling off the many decaying layers of skin above us to reveal a genuine goodness and freshness within

---

overfocus on this quality and become stuck instead in loops that do not serve us. When we veer off our course because we forget we are equally feminine, we are reminded that we need to manifest based on what information we are receiving from around us as well.

us that deserves another's attention. This grace is available to us and comes with honesty with ourselves and others. Grace emerges through prayer, service to others and self-care.

This book aims to guide each reader and show what happens when we unlock this spiritual evolutionary potential through my personal ascension journey.

There will come a time when 'solutions' to complex world problems no longer hold us back or repeat as dreadful, depressing narratives. The New World is calling for us to think differently. We are reminded of our divine nature - we are creative, whole and capable of a new chapter, which was always filled with hope, trust and safety whether we were privy to it or not. Many wisdom teachers, contemporary life coaches, and everyday heroes show us this reality. We must believe we are equally creative and worthy of an abundant, joyous, thriving life.

Even if there is this resignation that we are 'doomed' to mutually exclusive decisions and that the world is a zero-sum game. This is the outlook of realists who, unfortunately, govern and lead most organisations worldwide, and it could very well be you reading this book as well. Even if we were not like this before, culture and operating procedures can turn us into thinking and acting this way. How, then, do we overcome this mainstream rhetoric for now? Lean into our daily practices and beliefs, harness the energetic resonance of our heart-brain coherence to feel more love and synchronicity between our destiny and free will choices.

We are surrounded by illusions that either keep us stuck in fear or free us - *we get to choose.*

We want to avoid abandoning ourselves in this time of need. Self-betrayal is more commonplace than we would like to think and mainly stems from fear. It means walking away from our highest good because we think there is no way out or we cannot do it. We need to overcome this illusion to succeed in life. It will require us to step out of our comfort zones, see things as they are, and be accountable for ourselves in our thoughts, emotions, and speech. This will help us to end cycles of ignorant objectives steeped in disregard for ourselves. We live in a quantum world where every action and non-action counts towards manifesting our visions. We live in a living world where every action has a consequence. Understanding these laws can help us co-exist more harmoniously within Gaia. We need to begin by suspending our judgment of ourselves and others. Be kind, compassionate, and equally determined to make changes that serve the greater good. One person making one change makes a difference. Co-Prosperity requires this build-up of momentum.

We might still hesitate due to fear created by old, outdated programming. To proceed, **we need to meet this fear or worst-case scenario.** Fundamentally, fear is simply a mode of operating in this world. Its benefits include restrictions/limitations to narrow our options and, on the other hand, keep us safe. It stems from a survival mentality because alternatives were unavailable or not nearby in our history. Instead of having the freedom to entertain options, most of us were forewarned for wanting to venture beyond to keep us 'safe'. Some of its common trauma language[6] include and is not exclusive to: 'I told you so', 'What did I say about doing ...', 'Now see what you have done, there is nothing we can do about it now', etc. The good news is that we can understand the roots of fear, appreciate its purpose and let go if it no longer serves us. Times are different now. We can seed more supportive paradigms that allow innovative growth and risk-taking for our inner creativity to shine. This works as long as we recognise we are not in survival mode now. Self-empowerment will be vital as we learn to rally ourselves and others towards the most impactful changes for the collective. Our resolve to lead ourselves towards fulfilment and bliss needs to be firm, and when it is not, be patient until it comes through.

Further, we must also socialise ourselves into believing that there is no danger in stepping into the unknown. The anxiety of not knowing does not need to scare us. It can empower us when we trust that we are being guided from within us. This is a path no one else has taken, especially if you come from fraught ancestral lines ridden with conflict, pain and trauma. Being our new ancestor, we will be continuously tested to choose

---

6   *Trauma language refers to common phrases or words we tend to use when in the height of emotions and without realising it. When we are aware of what is our trauma language, we can start to heal that sentiment, emotion. We are not this language, and we can let it go lovingly. Please avoid self-judgment and hold space instead for the reason behind why the language is there in the first place.*

the highest good variable in any situation, even if it may initially seem to our detriment. Building our rock-solid resolve to be of service to more than ourselves will birth changemakers who bring a **whole** sense of balance to this world, which is genuinely remarkable. Wholeness cannot be self-righteous. It is not from a place of judging nor soliciting advice. Wholeness is the recognition that we have all suffered. We hold space for another. We allow their healing to unfold. We respect boundaries – theirs and ours. We know our boundaries, and we act responsibly. We recognise the power of our words and unexpressed thoughts and constantly purify them. We neither put ourselves nor others down. We are energetically aware of our limitations and that of others. We take control over how we feel, respond and think about situations, people and experiences. We heal, we let go, we move on. We communicate.

Wholeness will be our reward. This is because, at every moment, we were consistent in our choices, spoke clearly to the universe about our intentions, and made choices that aligned with them. Any fears that came up were offered to the higher realms to transmute and transform the way we once saw and experienced a 'painful' occurrence. We solved problems as they occurred and did not procrastinate on our divine roadmap. We took baby steps despite the fog, noise and clouded inner worlds. We respected and stuck to our paths with determined action to find a way. We were, are and will always be relentless in seeking the Truth that we are all eternally happy, peaceful and loving beings.

How will this be possible in our dualistic world? By using the exact lens of duality that makes us think we are separate from the whole, we can start to appreciate the silver linings in our painful experiences and welcome more trust, surrender and love into our lives instead. **We are meant to be imperfect**, but we will need to keep learning and internalising life lessons so that we can strengthen our personalities to move forward and show the way to others to regain our sense of our whole selves again. This is a realisation we will have as we ascend and meet our older versions each time we look back. During these moments, it is usual for one to wonder why they could not see the situation as they do now or how they could have acted as such.

Through this rejuvenation process, we must offer ourselves the same compassion we would to a dear friend. We might take flight, freeze or fight with ourselves as we encounter painful memories out of shame or embarrassment of our social conditioning. This is when we can tell ourselves we are meant to have these experiences to hone the beloved within – the eternal space beyond any right or wrong where unconditional love always exists – to paraphrase Rumi. We must not judge ourselves for we chose this because we know we can overcome its wrathful association that keeps us locked in self-hate. We have come to Earth to experience the unlocking of bliss when we allow wisdom to come through for us in these moments.

The more we surrender, the easier it will be to forge new neurological pathways and open up new channels for self-forgiveness and forgiveness of everyone else who may have hurt us, intentionally or unintentionally. Fear becomes less as we gain new insights into why we and others behave the way they do and how we used to react before gaining this new state of mind-heart resonance. We strengthen our unified field within ourselves to be more understanding with others. We eventually reconnect with all we once thought we lost or were incapable of.

Our experiences are not in isolation; they activate our leadership DNA to make sense and do something about them. Somewhere in the space-time continuum, someone else is experiencing a similar interlocution with themselves and feeling less alone because we are healing with them. We are accepting and reframing the 'issue' or 'fear'. To move ahead with a resilient resolve to no longer be 'victims' of our thoughts and emotions steeped in inherited or unfounded fears fuelled by unhealthy neurological pathways previously seeded when we were more susceptible. We empower ourselves when we make this monumental shift to recognise our humanity in this present moment.

What will it take to rejuvenate?

Many of our systems have needed redesign, and people have been reskilled or upskilled to complement automation trends. Where we lack resources, we are turning to newer commodities that may be less carbon-intensive in one regard but more in an upstream or downstream capacity, depending on which Greenhouse gas emissions' scope we are looking at. Our core processes have needed to pivot, and we are making the shifts as subtly as possible due to our institutional fear programming for business continuity plans. Our organisational transformation depends on our risk averseness and capacity to accommodate 'disruptive' concepts like dignity®. Incorporating divine feminine qualities of gratitude, nurturing, and yielding in our hyper-masculine cultures will require mindset and behavioural shifts, specifically from doing to being, embodying, and trusting.

By presencing change within and between organisations, each organisation can benefit from teams equipped with learning the science of rejuvenation through the dignity® approach to creatively manage any risk while ensuring sufficiency in data, knowledge and business-sensitive information to address complex strategy, operations and even customer-engagement-related issues. In this regard, we will be venturing courageously within, and its value cannot be understated. Gratitude— the art of appreciating each other and nurturing—the art of creating suitable environments for all to thrive—must be necessary to succeed at work and home. These two essential practices form the bedrock of the dignity® approach. It leads to tangible outcomes despite being perceived as intangible. It offers recurring yield in the form of lower turnover rates and higher stakeholder satisfaction, which are often overlooked or disregarded during our regular day-to-day operations or crises.

By showing up better, we expand possibilities that can emerge, no matter how stressful a situation. We breathe easier when we know we are not in control. We let go of control when we tell ourselves we are doing our best. We thrive when we take better care of ourselves and have holistic goals and outlooks. We are unshakeable when we live a meaning-filled life – one that has more profound connections with others and where we feel at one with everything around us. How we are currently experiencing our world is evolving. We are highly creative beings who, with focused intentions and use of resources, can shape the quantum field we are in to vibrate more beauty, harmony, joy and prosperity for everyone. This has happened, is happening and will grow in movement once we all begin the pathways back to ourselves. From this inner knowing, we can see what is truly significant to us and how we may preserve it as sacred. We will evolve into reverence of all things that sustain and support us, knowing we too can return this support with action, thoughts and deeds that support our well-being and that of others.

In sum, this book lies at the intersection of personal development, leadership, and integrating sustainable change management, preferably with an understanding of the multi-stakeholder value chains we are a part of. We are focused on one outcome: a climate-neutral economy, at minimum, striving to eventually be circular, with closed resource loops where we co-prosper together. Understanding the impact of our upstream and downstream contributions is necessary for this to occur. We are all connected, especially at the consumer level. We contribute to heavy greenhouse gas emissions by choosing products and services we purchase, use, and dispose of. Fast fashion, cheaper online goods, and intensive use of digital products have gripped us with the appeal of lower costs, instant gratification, and constant stimulation. This has kept us locked into frequency bands that do not serve our highest good, and our highest good is to evolve to be the best versions of ourselves.

Sustainable development is impossible without our personal and collective well-being, and we will not be well if we do not sustainably build our systems, organisations, and communities.

This book concludes with a clear call to action for us to **return to nature** – nature that surrounds, provides and guides us from moment to moment. An intelligence we have taken for granted and misused for too long now. It is equally a call for us to return to our true nature as loving, peaceful and happy souls. It calls us to integrate the natural world into our ways of being. Each chapter ahead has been written by invoking a relevant element, plant, animal, sound and chakra intelligence, as I returned to Nature and its intelligence myself - thank you.

PART I

LET'S CO-PROSPER TOGETHER

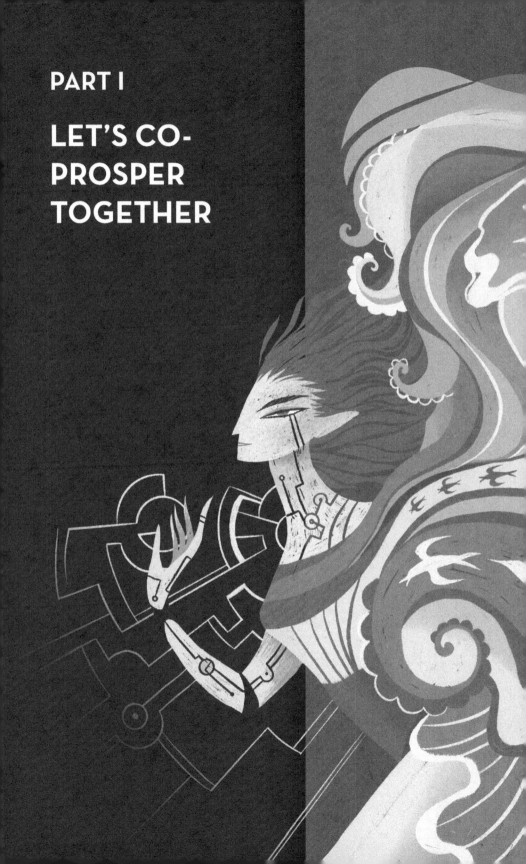

I

REWIRE THINKING

I n her book *Equity: How to Design Organizations Where Everyone Thrives,* Minal encourages those who feel threatened by the idea of sharing power to reconsider the compelling reasons for creating equitable systems. These systems aim to ensure everyone has the resources they need to succeed.[7] She also stresses the importance of 'accessibility' alongside promoting diversity, inclusion and equity. This ensures we enable systems and people to support each other in truly growing into a holistic network of stakeholders geared towards a common goal. Accessibility allows people in power to see how they influence opportunities for others and what they can do to create more so that everyone can thrive with their differences intact.

My personal story is one of structural, cultural and gendered limitations. I grew up in a working-class ethnic minority family who immigrated from Punjab before Singapore's independence, making me the second generation born and raised in Singapore. The rich-poor divide was a familiar rhetoric for unhappiness and the compulsive need to work doubly hard to make it in life. Having a good education was drilled into me from a young age, with studies being the only focal point of my existence. I was also born into probably the most competitive generational cohorts

---

7   M. Bopaiah, 'Equity: How to Design Organisations Where Everyone Thrives', Berett-Koehler Publishers, 9 August 2021 [audiobook].

in recorded Singapore history since it was the Dragon Year 1988. This is where the challenge emerged in terms of identity formation. Who was I besides the rat in a race I was unsure I wanted to be part of?

I did find snippets of what could be me in crisis moments when I was suddenly not doing well at school. This was the beginning of my experience of miracles, which I only realise now as I write this book.

It was 2004, and it began on a wonky note for me. Our school principal had suddenly passed on, and we went into mourning. Not knowing how I felt despite being interviewed by the Media and seeing classmates seek counselling for the grief, I remained numb to the entire episode. And I was close with my principal. She was a stern but kind woman who immediately saw my leadership potential when we met and ensured I maximised my abilities at her school. Time passed quickly that year as we skipped having mid-term examinations in light of what happened. Soon, the national examinations drew near, and I performed miserably in the lead-up. My mother was called in, and I was told I was dreaming if I thought I could make it to a tertiary institution. I stood there, well, you guessed it, numb.

Not one for emotional check-ins then, my mother went into action mode, and I committed to focus all my energy on the examinations, which were drawing near in two months. With no time to waste, I channelled all I had into studying. The morning of the examination was an early wake-up call for me as I was vomiting my dinner from the previous night. It came as mysteriously as it went, but I was all-round physically weak. I recall the 24-hour clinic giving me a jab and my father handing me an isotonic drink after another. This was THE national examination, and I had to make it. So, I managed to get to school with a doctor's note on my condition. The teachers thought including it with the examination script was a good idea, and I wrote the two-hour paper. After submitting the exam, I was in a better state and continued to press on for the upcoming ones.

Nervous jitters were all around when we stood in line to collect our results a few months later. I was resigned to whatever fate had in store because I had no benchmark. My parents did not complete high school. I was next in line and did not know what to expect since I had already witnessed the worst with the preliminary exams, and I did my best. I could handle some tough questions my peers struggled with when we discussed post-papers. I was still, very still. The person in front of me walks away, and I am staring at my teacher, who has a deadpan look on. He mutters, "I was not expecting this. You got 9 points. Congratulations!" and shakes my hands with this bewildered look, wondering how I managed to pull it off. I walked away to quickly take a look as I could not believe it either. My dream had come true – I managed six distinctions and will have a star with my name on a pillar. It happened. Thank you, but what's next?

We are all bound imaginarily to the sacred threads of divine clockwork that manifest the experiences we need to understand, heal and ascend out of our environments as lotus flowers or water lilies emerge from murky depths of stagnant ponds. But we need to put in the effort. We need to meet ourselves at every point instead of numbing or dissociating. There is no room for nonchalance if we wish to achieve the quantum leaps to transformative leadership within our families, organisations and communities. I learnt this as I braced through every experience that seemed 'unattainable'.

What is within us that we must disconnect from and let go of to move forward towards our dreams?

I quickly realised that it was my dualistic nature that I had to overcome. Like many other experiences that preceded that poignant memory of 2004, I oscillated between numbness and anger. Or a combination of two opposing emotions, which I later learnt is not something to feel guilty for. Instead, I had to learn to sublimate these opposing feelings to unite them and decide what I wanted to make of my life. For instance, anger in a moment may be related to an 'injustice', 'unfairness', etc, and it always presents us with a choice regarding what we want to do about it.

We can only expect results based on what we are investing in.

In this age of transformation, we will have to rewire our thinking to find the middle ground in everything, as it is so easy to get swept away in polarising rhetoric. Sometimes, it requires more energy from our conscious mind; other times, it requires making this a learnt habit so that we can evolve.

When we believe we are all part of one consciousness, we can be grateful for every perceived positive or negative situation because we can use what we 'dislike' in another person or what they are mirroring to keep expanding our consciousness. What we notice in someone else that makes us uncomfortable might just as well be part of our shadow aspect unknown to us. We will need to reach a state of non-reaction to know that we have integrated our shadow aspects. Till then, we can reframe these uncomfortable encounters to quantum leap forward. In turn, we can hold space for others as we see ourselves in them.

We allow things to happen as they need to and learn how we navigate these challenges because we start to believe we can. We let go of victim mindsets and accept that this is life on Earth. Through these reminders, we are rewiring our neurological pathways and inviting more light into our circumstances and lives. This will be constantly revolving as this is a dynamic planet where everyone's action has an impact, and we build our awareness to ensure we always see things as they are instead of what we wish they were. We must also believe that neither positive nor negative thinking is 'good or bad'. It just is, and we can overcome black-and-white thinking through self-forgiveness and acceptance. As we persistently work away at reconciling our mental and emotional perspectives that label and make us overthink and worry, we contribute to our evolution to achieve a zero-mind state.

Knowing what can challenge us to hone this ability is crucial, as well as learning how to mitigate and adapt accordingly, especially if our jobs require us to be exposed to them. For example, there are tendencies in our social media to force-feed us, either positive or negative messaging, to make us FEEL better or worse. We might also start comparing ourselves and feel this 'lack' within us even if no one told us so. Understanding what emerges when we expose ourselves to such influential domains is helpful if we observe and integrate what we learn about ourselves to ensure we do not fall susceptible to that feeling again.

The only source that can help us evolve towards happiness is within our sacred heart space, the temple of our physical being. It takes me a long while to understand what this means, and it began with a health crisis, as it does with most of us who might not understand or know evolution is knocking on our door for our spiritual growth that is due. It takes me seeking many experiences overseas and in various spiritual modalities to understand that the community and communion I seek are within me.

If we cannot sit with ourselves to experience this, we miss out on an essential aspect of our multidimensional experience here on Earth. Firstly, we are souls having a human experience before we are humans. Remembering and connecting with our essence is where we feel safest, protected, and guided. It begins again with believing that life presents us with more miracles than we acknowledge. Each time someone is kind to us, we get to smile at another, or there is a positive atmosphere, leaving us feeling good inside out; that is a miracle. A miracle that helps us remember this can be our moment-to-moment reality if we evolve.

Besides regarding our physical body as a temple, we benefit from constantly dropping into our heart space. We know this feeling when we have a heart-to-heart connection with someone who makes our hearts glow and reminds us of our inner goodness. The sacred heart is without agenda and conditions. It is divine love embodied. We wish all beings to be well and not harm ourselves and others. We live in loving grace every moment, being gentle with ourselves and others.

It is, therefore, essential to respect our sacred heart and acknowledge its emerging feelings as signposts for our journey instead of internalising messaging from around us. Happiness in this book refers to taking steps towards growth to open to our unique abilities and talents. It is a complete surrender to birthing New Earth through our sacred contribution to its evolution. It may require some of us to show up differently from others, and we need to accept that there is no shame, lack or embarrassment.

We are all worthy. This is a message that I have had to explain to myself over and over again as I shifted in and out of my career. I constantly sought growth compared to my ancestors, who had worked for a single employer for most of their lives. The importance of making the most of my time here on Earth and unravelling all the gifts available for my flourishing was just too important, and I felt guilty about this pursuit until recently. Until I recognised and appreciated the many sacrifices and delayed gratifications it took to reach this point. As a female in a predominantly patriarchal culture, I am an outlier, and to achieve what I have takes a tremendous amount of courage, which I acknowledge now.

Stepping out of intergenerational trauma, inherited fear patterns, as well as comfort zones is not easy. I am thankful that it has helped me meet new people, gain novel experiences, and expand my knowledge domains.

Individuals who have realised this inner power know how much pain and turmoil has occurred on Earth because we choose to stay stuck to our external worlds instead of turning inward.

In this journey towards evolution, turning inward is understandably scary because we are either afraid of being alone, left behind or vulnerable to the inner unknown workings of our mind. The self-critic is usually the first element we must address when attempting to rewire our thinking. Who is this inner voice? And is it ours in the first place? The second element we have to manage is our ego-mind, and for those of us in life roles where we have had to manage others, be it their temper, expectations or demands, we understand that our ego-mind is no different. It often pops into our consciousness with comments that challenge us whenever we steer towards our hearts as though to "caution" us of something bad that is to happen. And even if this is not to happen, thanks to the pure potentiality of our minds, we are likely to manifest it, creating a reassuring loop for our limiting beliefs to continue building upon.

We must acknowledge, accept, and thank these internalised voices in our heads for their unsolicited advice and well-intentioned fear-mongering, which contribute to our indecisive decision-making because, ironically, it helps us eventually to turn inwards for clarity. We have to thank it for making us feel emotionally unsafe to seek solutions that remind us to go inward because we are all figuring out our ways. We are our prophets. When we accept responsibility for our choices, thanks to our sacred heart, we usher in a new way of being. We can begin to rewire our thinking by adopting a kinder, more reassuring and supportive voice – much like picking the accents for Siri on your iPhone.

What may have been seen as scary or unnerving, which we may have overcompensated with our ego projections, can melt away. We are set free of ego's false grips of fear and can start to embrace our true selves again. This is homecoming. The only fear that appears is from our ancestors who did not get a chance, who lived in different circumstances and are looking out for us in their ways. And we can commune with them to honour their journeys and set them free. We can let them know that times are different now, and while we face similar challenges, we choose to heal and forgive. To end the vicious cycles so that our family lines can thrive now.

In this transformation era, many awakened individuals are working with local communities to use natural resources more sustainably to ensure livelihoods and environment restoration can ensure co-prosperity for as long as possible. Others are embedded in all types of organisations, from universities to governments and corporations, to help smoothen the transitions needed with their heart-based, integrity-conscious leadership. Like them, we too can awaken to ignite the movement towards this New World. Envisioning the New Earth will require inter-linkages with Nature and new social norms through this book and many others as thought leaders arise. We will need to move past pure extraction and transaction.

Practising gratitude for our ecology will require deeper resonance and optimisation. *Beyond protecting our interests, how can we assure the well-being of all through our due diligence processes?*

How may we connect our intelligence systems to be more people-centric? Are we respecting people's right to information, and is the data accurate?

Where may we give back more to the natural world to restore and rejuvenate their ecosystems, more directly – beyond partner programmes, co-benefits from carbon offset projects, etc?

What alliances are we nurturing within our organisations to form a network of experts or to develop a network of solutions to support the incubation of ideas to market?

How may we contribute to socialising the success and failure of circular economic initiatives so that they can continue despite challenges?

What tangible benefits can we receive from establishing interdependent and complimentary partnerships developed from mapping the macro and micro-trade-offs within our industries?

Lastly, how may we yield longevity of our systems? By longevity, we refer to the self-organising, self-correcting and self-sustaining characteristics of Nature:

Consciousness is everything. The dualistic aspect of human nature needs to be acknowledged as we kickstart this book with the intention towards a conscious journey into our personal self-realisation. We aim to strengthen our unified field of consciousness within ourselves to help birth new realities on Earth that will support the co-prospering of every being, leaving no one behind. In this unity consciousness, all seeking eventually ends, and we live for love, which becomes a frequency band within our very human body. There is no separation or entanglement. We remember the feeling of trust, and we trust the good and evil. We dissolve like water and let go of all attachments, self-imposed limitations, and socially conditioned viral programming based on fear. We learn to help others by holding space and loving them unconditionally. We let them see all of us and allow ourselves to be empty and whole simultaneously. We remember we only need love, not help or advice.

Our first book, 'The Action Gap: Business Strategies for Co-Prosperity', referenced our shadow side and the inner alignment needed to lead with dignity and consciousness. It first requires each leader to know and accept themselves in all totality. This includes the painful, awkward and self-deprecating moments of truth we impose on ourselves or allow others to do so on our behalf. This is a requirement for recognising our humanity and that of others. It sees ourselves as equals and worthy of respect, freedom, acceptance and trust. We are only truly happy when we can be honest and authentic with ourselves and each other.

Values will be integral to the awakening towards dignity consciousness. Values serve as important guidance for us to be consistent in our behaviour, avoid self-betrayal, and make decisions with integrity and trust so that we can all thrive as a just society. Within organisations, values help create positive work environments that offer motivation and successful contributions toward all realms of sustainability. We often judge ourselves and others. We allow ourselves to hold on to the lenses and constructs of who we are when our eternal nature is the pure essence of a lotus flower rising above murky waters. By what we believe and how we think and act, we allow ourselves to stay deep in the murky waters, never to emerge. Those who do cannot see themselves as beautiful flowers due to the lack of clear, reflective waters around them. This leaves cuts in our psyche, and tremendous healing is required to merge back into all that is, which we often disregard, especially if we still depend on our surroundings to show us who we are.

Until self-actualisation, we will continue in this never-ending cycle of unconscious co-creation, competitive greed, and jealous comparison. If we remain dormant in these truths, we inevitably contribute to chaos. If the Garden of Eden and pure potentiality are within us all, imagine how much less we will be worried, anxious, scared, and angry when something or someone is taken from us. We can move on and continuously progress because we know one thing or someone is not the be-all and end-all of life. We have the conscious choice to choose better, make anew, and attract more fruitful relationships and outcomes.

While the consensus behind the nature and origin of consciousness is still evolving, some theories "suggest it arises from complex brain processes, while others propose it might be a fundamental property of the universe".[8]

Regardless, this book calls on all of us to connect with our higher consciousness, for it is an empowerment medicine. Awakening our consciousness and its vastness allows us to constantly expand our awareness of what is happening around us, how it affects us internally, and what we can do to solve problems and improve things. Consciousness has other names, such as creative intelligence or higher intelligence. It is as mysterious as it is tangible, and many of us often experience its expansion when we are called to make changes to flow with the way of the Tao, the universal flow. Given our preference to control and be certain of outcomes, we might not recognise the power within this flow and might end up resisting or resenting it instead. When we accept it as it is, our consciousness often becomes our greatest teacher and guide in our integration journey with our multifaceted self.

On this path, **maturity, inner strength and ascension are the fruits we reap from seeking Truth**, purifying our old selves and rising above the illusions that surround us daily. Unfortunately, many of us are deluding ourselves into staying status quo thanks to fear-based programming we inherited before birth. The ancestral coding for some of us who come from intergenerational trauma patterns or vicious cycles of poverty and addiction, for example, further fuels this fear. These inherited traits shape our personality and relationships by affecting our trust in ourselves and others. It impacts the level of transformation we can witness by either keeping us stuck or helping us to be resilient in the storm of changes evident in this journey. By transmuting unhelpful emotional, psychological and behavioural patterns, we may address these deep-seated sequences in our genomes to birth new possibilities by connecting with our consciousness.

This is fundamental understanding for any of us who wants to thrive at what we do in the real world. Our experiences, especially in our foundational years, make us today's leaders. A good leader can bring

---

[8]   M. Hudson, Psychology Today, 'What Actually Is Consciousness, And How Did It Evolve?', 7 October 2023, https://www.psychologytoday.com/us/blog/finding-purpose/202009/what-actually-is-consciousness-and-how-did-it-evolve (Accessed 6 September 2024).

others along, including our family and co-workers. With so much change invariably needing us to show up better, the task of a regulator, corporate executive and community leader today calls for superhero-like yielding to ensure the collective good can be achieved and maintained no matter what. How to best uphold the spirit of justice and promote collective harmony is not intrinsically found in the blueprint of most of our contemporary governance systems. We are instead trying to stay afloat with our largely segmented and defensive structures from the terror and invasion that has historically pervaded our private and public lives through time and space. For example, not knowing how to deal with the proliferation of a scalable technology would naturally create closed, defensive structures that limit the human potential to transcend beyond structures. Instead, we begin to think we need more structures to enforce harmony and peace when it is further dividing us and causing fear, paranoia and deep-seated resentment towards one another.

A system built on dignity consciousness naturally weeds out the harmful effects of any technology created to monopolise, hegemonise and overrule collective will present in any space. It enables and holds space for diversity of opinions without needing to rule over anyone or ensure one precedes another. No one feels threatened, isolated or marginalised. This system thrives on a social contract and ethos, prioritising co-creation for our highest good. We still have some time to reach this point, and we might be able to realise it sooner than expected should we all prioritise our ascension journeys.

It will require us to overcome our indifference to the challenges of our systems by achieving self-mastery and being versatile to the changing needs of our economic systems. When we do so, we can make quantum leaps towards heart-based transactions that put dignity at the fore. Dignity consciousness has a rights-based focus. It recognises that many segments of our societies have unequal access to funds due to inherited money blueprint challenges, systemic discrimination such as bias and insufficient level playing fields to ensure widespread financial knowledge and intergenerational wealth accumulation. This can change with a values-based approach focused on co-prosperity, not profit and returns margins alone.

Our systems, therefore, need to bring humanity *back* into its dynamic functioning.

In ancient times, consultative governance and procedural justice mechanisms ensured healing at its root source and authentic community organising that celebrates the unique identities and traditions of different collective entities within a society. Although this may still be practised in some parts of the world within Indigenous communities and more populous nations like India that require decentralised village-level governance, the procedural justice manner of operating is largely based on how to avoid, punish or separate a threat from the general public rather than 'how to heal this from the root source'.

How can communities unaffected by urbanisation and the need for higher-income jobs keep thriving to uphold their culture and traditions that resonate with Nature?

Infrastructure losses caused by extreme weather patterns are a stark example of how easily displaced we can be. To acclimatise to changing weather patterns, we need to build our homes in synchronicity with our environments using nature-based solutions or local building materials and techniques. When we overload a machine, it responds with either a malfunction or breakdown, right? Similarly, our appetite for consistent and constant development requires a review. Going forward, we will likely face further disruptions if we maintain business as usual. The good news is that bad actors and bottom-up developments are making us evolve and adapt, but mainly from a reactive and defensive stance. What if we could reframe our approach to one of unifying systems not for central control but from a standpoint of being **antifragile**? No matter the 'harm-inducing' incidents, the system quickly learns and counteracts with its advanced intelligence algorithm fed by all systems connected to it, making it the literal heart of a governing entity. Our first book shares how sustainability management systems can leverage chaos theory to become antifragile.

Here, fear no longer presides. We are safe and protected by a defensible system that can grow and manage itself in self-reliant ways, feeding into the tributaries of communities and securing accurate and timely communications to keep everyone informed. The human resilience to expand our consciousness to rise above these arbitrary trappings of our lives will matter the most. Only when we raise our consciousness to see things as they are, overcome powerlessness, and own what we can know do we operate undisrupted in this world. Nothing and no one can shake us anymore, and we no longer blame others. We no longer misuse our power by giving it away or taking it from someone else. We no longer stay stuck or repeat unhealthy patterns. We no longer displace our pain onto others.

We step into our true destiny, which is the evolution towards an inner happiness that is self-organising and regenerative without needing external validation or impetus. It is an ever-flowing fountain of light and progressive thinking within us that helps us create and contribute in unimaginable ways. This book calls for all of us to return to our very nature—the ever-generous, creative, and fulfilling life force that sustains the entire cosmos and Mother Earth. Power, purity, knowledge, and childlike play become our natural state. We create not for the sake of but for the betterment of all. We are responsible for ourselves. We recognise we are not a singular aspect of this universe but part of a collective whole. As we embark on our healing journeys, this will become a reality. We become transformative leaders with goals to remember and reunite ecology and economy. To some degree, we know this. We all know too well the effects of too much development at the cost of our communities, especially those limited by access and opportunities. We see the impact on how we treat our air quality, water streams and food production systems. The repercussions on our public health are increasingly noticeable now, with unfortunate consequences for the younger generations, from rising asthma cases to poor lung capacities due to unaddressed air pollution.

These issues cannot be disregarded any more.

Those of us who are unsure or in denial are starting to at least feel its effects through extreme weather patterns or food shortages in various markets, as shown in periodic supply chain disruptions. We are awakening to the need to at least fend ourselves from these potential risks and impacts. Those of us with access to capital and markets face higher costs and premiums on green or more sustainable commodities, and those who lack access in the first place potentially face starvation and nutritional deficits, especially children.

Just as individuals become more aware of and adopt ecological principles in their personal lives, organisations can also become more attuned to them. By integrating concepts like biomimicry—where strategies and solutions are inspired by nature—into their planning and operations, organisations can enhance how they strategise, optimise their processes, and ensure long-term sustainability for their business operations that might impact local communities. Moving forward, businesses will likely be donning the hat of regulators, too. Enforcing climate compliance on our suppliers to meet consumer demands for more ethical products and services will grow increasingly common. The sooner we start thinking of our co-prosperity models, the better we will be from a business sustainability point of view.

This also applies to governments and social agencies. Our financial systems and governance models operate on debt financing, which is not sustainable if we continue to experience more disruptions and need upfront investments to lessen the shock of fiscal requirements and avoid social crises. What is a realistic and much-needed constructivist take on an appropriate co-prosperity model requires a whole-of-society approach to addressing the multidimensionality of our crises today. We have been largely indifferent to the co-dependencies within our systems without realising how it cripples us and, in turn, affects our social fabric. Those of us in the systems who see this shortfall only grow more indifferent to the point of hopelessness because of a multi-actor, multi-operational and multi-agency effort that will be required to identify the whole elephant, accept it and transform inside-out based on a non-partisan participatory approach. This will take a miracle for us, much like how the global community galvanised to arrange for vaccines to be administered at the heights of a pandemic in 2021. The fact that most of our societies still depend on non-profit and charitable contributions to facilitate the survival of marginalised groups calls for a dignity crisis.

How may we review how we use our funds to secure basic needs while creating new opportunities for all to thrive?

Figure 1 shows 'balance' as one of the five central aspects of co-prosperity. These five aspects are North Stars, guiding us to establish systems, organisations, and teams to contribute to the New Earth.

- **'Balance'** refers to the equitable use of resources with the regeneration of living ecosystems as a goal. It also refers to a holistic geospatial metrics system that can track the indicators of our air and water, similar to seismic activity. It requires the reparations from truth and reconciliation models to be applied to ensure previously exploited economies are owed their dues to rebuild better. Balance requires considering the other, the environment and how we manage corruption at the individual and societal level. Corruption here refers to morals as much as it does monetary. It relates to how we betray ourselves when not walking the talk, aligned with our values or considering the greater good. Here, the greater good refers to the evolutionary progress we must commit to for us all to thrive. It is often mistaken as humanitarian aid or government handouts when it is about a systemic adoption and implementation of dignity consciousness rooted in equitable structures.

- **'Sustenance'** refers to viable agricultural methods that ensure soil, land, and animals can naturally support population growth and development. Localisation and managing carbon footprinting of transportation of produce will also be crucial components as we move forward, not as curbs to international trade but as a responsible acknowledgement of what sustains us and who is playing the biggest role in this. Farmers are one of the most underserved classes of workers globally, and they need to be included in re-evaluating our commodity pricing markets and the value we are pegging for food security. Like high occupational hazard roles, farmers need support to grow their sector and invest in decarbonising their operations. Coupled with more downstream awareness of our waste management systems – how are we polluting our Earth with what we dispose of? Where is our waste landing? Which ecosystems are we destroying, and how can we do better to ensure we do not further harm the ecosystem services that many of our industries, especially food supplies, rely on?

- 'Spiritual evolution' refers to our inevitable destiny on Earth. As we realise the stark duality of our time, the deeper our longing will get to rise above these illusions to uncover the true nature of our beings and this world. As we do our inner work, the more we will meet with the light that will transform our gene codes to make us born anew as whole beings ready to serve the collective whole with humility, groundedness and passion to reach elevated solutions and progress for the totality of our existence. To avoid climate litigation claims and inauthentic business trajectories, we must transmute the vibrations holding us back due to ignorance or fear. These need not be giant leaps of transformation. Many quantum leaps through conscious thought and action eventually lead to Gardens of Eden all around us. As creative and conscious beings, we can gracefully co-create harmony within and around us at all times.

- 'Ethical conduct' refers to honouring healthy boundaries and respecting our rights to self-realisation. Our personal sovereignty will never harm another if we are mindful of our ethical standards and are spiritually evolved. We will know how to respect others as we respect ourselves. Reaching this point will require conscious efforts to self-reflect where we may be experiencing a story of 'lack' and transmute it to an abundance mindset. Growing in love and wisdom will require forgiveness, mercy, and humility. As we spiritually evolve, the conscious effort to treat others with dignity becomes paramount. This is because we inevitably start seeing the other from a soul consciousness basis rather than a form basis. At the soul-to-soul level, we are all one: unity personified. The vibrational dissonance of being on Earth has made us forget our true selves, which presents an opportunity for us to evolve.

- 'Economy of well-being' refers to a macro, meso and micro shift in how we value commodities, money and time. Earth, as a planet, is a living being, and the human body is a fascinating receptacle of meridian points and energy centres. The more we return to nature and start recognising what is truly sustaining us, the more we realise the harms imposed upon us by the structures and lifestyles manifested from focusing on self-neglect through over-working, working in wrong conditions and/or earning through inappropriate means. Well-being needs to be an indicator of true value creation moving forward. And anything that takes away time from us needs to be devalued. Productivity has to be a key focus in this transition, where we free up time for humans to seek spiritual evolution for the greater good, in this case, societal growth. At the individual level, we will all be challenged to shift our approach and focus from money as a lifestyle or material goods provider to an enabler of dreams. We all have a unique dream to execute on Earth. Many have forgotten. We are here to create Heaven on Earth, precisely where we are at right now.

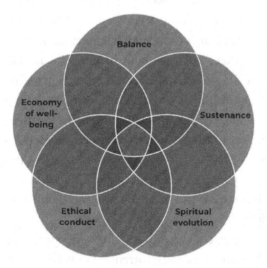

Figure 1: Co-Prosperity is a holistic approach that redefines what wealth means to us at an individual, organisational and societal level

Such an effort would require longer political terms than we practice and, most importantly, conscious and awake non-partisan leaders who see the big picture while walking the talk. Where are these unicorns? They are around. Most are doing their best back-end, fighting fires that "unexpectedly" emerge from the negative feedback loops of these systems, only to be too tired to be seen or heard with their problem-solving insights. Or, if heard, faced with further obstacles to test their resolve. Some give up and leave the institutions, while others adapt and keep their heads low. But these unicorns are around.

A whole systems approach by various multi-stakeholder coalitions will be required to make this monumental shift alongside spiritual evolutions at the individual level. Once our inner worlds are cleared out of their outdated stories and energetic imprints, we will naturally start co-creating a co-prosperous world from the bottom up, especially supporting top-down systems change towards a profound progression in human history. This will not be without its upheavals. We will need to invest in consistent efforts towards our highest evolutionary growth. We will also need to shift from a capitalist to a gift economy, where we re-evaluate how we transact and what delivers true value instead.

Many reasons can explain how we got here. The main challenge has been that because most of our societies were feudalistic before we became the democratic or semi-unconsolidated democracies that we are today, we have imperfect market structures built by elites for personal gain, given the contextual social 'agreements' of those times. Throw in contemporary power nexus relationships - while the share of the pie grew with the inclusion of a few more actors, this has remained a largely zero-sum game for the rest of society until new wealth owners through big data, emerging technology and highly scalable start-up venture investing showed up. Even then, the pie may have grown larger, with a select few still enjoying the slice. This is just how the structure was and continues to be from an objective standpoint.

Since this book calls for reunifying how we operate and how nature functions, it will require accepting current states with their shadow aspects, which we largely avoid. By consistently moving towards the desired state, no matter how challenging, we can begin to unburden systems. This path is not for the weak-willed or opportunists. It is for the committed who understand that we can no longer take more than we give and everything always comes to balance (sometimes we can understand this, while other times it will be a mystery – almost like an ancestral/*karmic* debt that is due or owed).

As we understand, cycles are flows of being that occur when we set off a particular intention or step into a pattern that we either inherit or create through our actions, words and thoughts that can harm or slow us down. These cycles can look very different. A seemingly prosperous cycle of material wealth can deplete the very life force energy out of us if we are curtailing an aspect of ourselves from showing up at the table and vice versa. Similarly, overemphasising any one aspect of our multi-dimensional self could create imbalances in our growth cycles that can create stress or lethargy in our physiology – namely, nervous and parasympathetic systems.

This, in turn, disrupts our lifestyle, health, and overall well-being when we cannot be present in total health and consciousness.

Evolutionary growth refers to the body as much as it does the mind and spirit. Until we heal these aspects of our genealogy, we remain cut off from the higher evolutionary gene codes available to us through light and energetic downloads. The reader accepts that we are walking energetic systems deeply connected to the quantum field of possibilities through our thoughts, actions, and words. When we heal our physical system through mental and emotional inner work, we activate our spiritual quotient for intuitive strengths and access to higher truths evident in our current reality. We start seeing things as they are and respond instead of reacting. We are calmer and more compassionate to others because we understand their suffering. We forgive more easily because we were once where they were at.

This heart-based opening requires a deep courage to uncover all that has been dissociated from us through our shadow aspects. It requires us to unite opposites within ourselves, which also extends to external situations relating to our principles. It will require us to follow our *dharma*, which many have been too scared or in denial about. We each have specific life purposes to heal ourselves, our families and our communities. And as we heal, we heal the whole. This beautiful synarchy cannot happen when we are numb, avoidant or indifferent. It begins when we start feeling and offering creative solutions to bring harmony, peace and well-being to all, including animals.

New Earth mindsets require firstly that we acknowledge our inherent nature to contradict, sabotage, and upend our own lives with the decisions and choices we make based on how we feel, think, and act when we are unconscious or unaware. Here, we also reference the unprocessed emotional and psychological states known as *samskaras*. These act as compounding blocks to our current life challenges if not tackled or addressed simultaneously with our physical healing. These behaviours, habits, thought patterns, and emotional pain have locked us in the lower frequencies of scarcity, fear, and retribution. By identifying our respective genetic and spiritual ancestral patterns in our shadow, we can transmute and unlock our self-mastery. Here, we remember that darkness is of the light, for we would not know its existence without the absence of light.

The good news is that if we begin healing from expanding our consciousness, we address *all* the realms of our energetic bodies—*mental, emotional, physical, and spiritual.*

Regarding inter-relational interactions and community building, we need to experience being one with Nature at the individual level. This is where we can start rewriting our stories by reconciling the past, offering suitable reparations, repairing the present with healing, and recalibrating our lifestyle with holistic priorities that support, nourish, and guide us towards a meaningful life. Here, we can reimagine our futures and rejuvenate outcomes that serve a greater whole. While an economic approach has helped us with its quantifiable metrics and theories, we must now shift to an eco-spiritual approach. This refers to how best we recognise the interlinkages between the water, fire, metal, earth, and air elements around us. As we raise our consciousness, we can connect to learn and respect the life force that exists in us all as it does in Nature.

Similarly, we may use dignity consciousness to change the course of our hyper-driven masculine modus operandi across our organisations to ensure more equitable, inclusive and empowered conversations and outcomes with our stakeholders. The intention is to harness heart-based leadership that helps us see where we might be 'losing out' regarding authentic communications and how we may achieve balance with what we are 'gaining'.

The dignity® approach can offer a step-by-step guide through this business transformation process:

Figure 2: Trademark registered with the
Intellectual Property Office of Singapore

Due Diligence: To begin, we must examine our current business operations models. We could ask ourselves: *What opportunities exist to close our resource loops?*

Have we considered circular economy options like remanufacturing, recycling, recovery, servitisation, the sharing economy, and designing for longevity?

Reflecting on past initiatives, we must identify what worked and what did not, enabling us to learn and adapt for future success. Next, we must analyse how we organise our workflows with **I**ntelligence. *Are there processes that can be optimised further?*

Identifying areas where our team needs time to catch up with work can reveal opportunities for improvement. Additionally, we could explore ways to enhance learning and evaluate the role of technology in our operations. *Are we using the right platforms to maximise the efficiency and effectiveness of what we need to achieve?*

Actively practising **g**ratitude can help us celebrate success and appreciate the moments that did not work as well. This is because we focus on the efforts, not outcomes, over which we have limited control. Acknowledging our people through their conscientious work fosters a positive organisational culture. *We could reflect on what we can be grateful for in the past year, particularly regarding planned behaviours within our organisation.*

Are we receiving appropriate stakeholder feedback, and can we do more to improve our thinking about our processes?

Celebrating small wins and gaining insights about initiatives that did not meet expectations or go as planned help us understand where we may have had blind spots and how we may more realistically or tangibly move forward to generate outcomes rather than outputs. The fact remains that change is a constant; chaos is to be expected, and our only way to resilience is to ensure we are anchored to ethical principles and ways of being that can carve out spaces for us to last through challenging times.

Along our ascension journeys, we will likely have uncomfortable conversations with others about what we deem ethical or not. Following are some conversational insights on how we may approach each other with dignity and calmness to understand more than label or judge so that we may grow together:

1. **Stay Calm and Collected**: Before addressing the issue, take a moment to compose yourself. Emotions can run high, and staying calm can help you communicate more effectively.

2. **Gather Facts**: Make sure you understand the situation fully. Gather any evidence or specific examples of unethical behaviour to support your claims.

3. **Choose the Right Time and Place**: Find a private and neutral setting to discuss the behaviour. This will help prevent defensiveness and promote a more open conversation.

4. **Express Your Concerns**: Use "I" statements to communicate how the behaviour affects you or others. For example, "I noticed that [specific behaviour], and it made me feel [your feelings]."

5. **Be Direct but Respectful**: Clearly articulate the unethical behaviour, but do so respectfully. Avoid personal attacks; focus on the actions instead.

6. **Encourage Reflection**: Ask questions, encouraging the person to reflect on their behaviour. For instance, "What were you thinking when you did that?" or "How do you think this affects others?"

7. **Suggest Alternatives**: If appropriate, offer constructive alternatives or solutions. This shows you're interested in helping them improve rather than just criticizing.

8. **Know When to Escalate**: If the behaviour continues or poses a serious ethical issue, consider reporting it to a supervisor, HR, or a relevant authority, depending on the context.

9. **Follow-Up**: If you feel comfortable, check in with the person later to see if they have reflected on the conversation or made any changes.

10. Take Care of Yourself: These discussions can be draining. Ensure you care for your well-being, especially if the situation is ongoing.

Ethical conduct involves exhibiting integrity and having a clear conscience. It supports building trust and stronger rapport with our stakeholders.

Consistent nurturing practices will also help us and others feel more empowered to understand the mission of contributing to sustainability. Some ideas include lunch talks by local eco-leaders or organisations and team-building activities in Nature, such as forest bathing and beach clean-ups. *List an initiative to get started on right away that does not cost much:*

We must assess where we invest our time and whether these investments yield high-impact returns. Engaging stakeholders and fostering a supportive environment can drive meaningful change. Practising illumination can help us embrace lifelong learning, which is crucial for growth and innovation. We can ask ourselves: *are we open to sharing and transcending the status quo to be more resourceful with what we have?*

Identifying valuable sources of information and benchmarking systems can help us measure performance and track progress within the industry or globally. This openness to learning and improvement is key to long-term success. Planning for long-term, tangible outcomes helps us focus on achieving our sustainability goals. Defining clear goals and documenting their progress is instrumental. It is important to clearly define what we aim to deliver with our change initiatives. By documenting successful pivots and sharing results with key stakeholders, we may leverage effective communication channels to ensure the transparency and accountability required for longstanding trust.

Rewiring our thinking to create an all-rounded impact will require adopting a dignity® creative solutions approach, where we may make a more sustainable and resilient future for our organisations. This transition is significant because we are advancing digitally and towards a nature-positive future. We will need to ensure the technological trade-offs are balanced with due considerations for environment, society, and governance issues as well (refer to Figure 3). As our final step in co-creating sustainable practices for our organisations, **y**ield ensures we consider the potential to reap climate, nature, social, and economic co-benefits.

If these benefits are not immediately apparent, what is our phased approach, and what are their associated timelines?

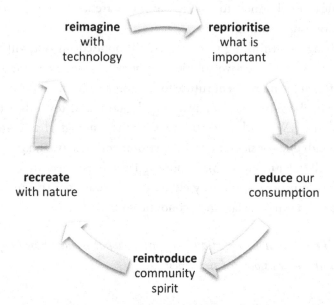

Figure 3: Five broad strokes needed to respect the sacred in our personal lives and with each other while rebuilding back better for nature and future generations to thrive

As cosmic beings, we heal in multifaceted ways, including sound (e.g., vibration), light, colours, physical inputs (e.g., filtered water, pure spring water, organic and nourishing food), and energy healing. The primordial sound of 'Sa' reverberates our detached and omniscient connection with the eternal consciousness of the cosmos. When strung with the other sounds, we invoke a cellular recognition of our spiritual affinity to the fundamental mantra for all healing and beingness: Ra Ma Da Sa Sa Say So Hung.[9] We start to remember more and more. This act of speaking, humming, and chanting activates our throat chakra, further influencing our state of oneness with all that is so that we may resonate at a higher vibration that assures us of its infinitely loving presence regardless of what may seem to be occurring around us.

---

[9] Yogapedia, *What is Ra Ma Da Sa Sa Say So Hung?*, 21 December 2023, https://www.yogapedia.com/definition/10604/ra-ma-da-sa-sa-say-so-hung (Accessed 31 May 2024).

We must tune in like a radio station and stay on this frequency band to realise we are _always_ supported, held and guided.

Here, Rooster wisdom is helpful – they know their identity and territory well. They consistently stand tall and are willing to fight another when it comes to it. There is an unshakeable gravitas about them, and they are formidable. This description shows how both its light and dark elements contribute to their personal power. Honing this wisdom can help us protect what is sacred from actors who feel financially limited or unable to move past pre-set mental models to preserve what we need to. We can embody the rooster energy to articulate the shifts that need to occur and assure ourselves that 'fear is safe'. Fear is an essential part of living, and we can respond positively to it with thoughtful reflections and mindful actions that are loving and kind to ourselves first and foremost.

The element of air helps purify our mental body – how we think, why we think the way we do and how we can shapeshift the contrasting bits of our thoughts, especially when doubt shows up to fuel ruminating thoughts like an unwanted YouTube ad. Repeating the affirmation 'fear is safe' can further bolster this practice as we learn to eventually reach a state of heart-brain coherence where thoughts are no longer necessary as we are guided by our heart. From this space, only love exists as we open our chakra for more light to pour in and activate our dormant Spiritual DNA to embody unconditional love. Here, fear no longer has a hold on us as we can meet it with compassion and assure it that it can let go. We are safe.

When we remember in such an intimate way, and each of us will have our unique awakening or 'aha' or 'nirvana' moment, we experience divine bliss consciousness. It guide us through this revival to help us take on the leadership mantle in our personal lives and fly high and confidently in pursuing our dreams. As keen watchers of the horizon, we can spot opportunities and make swift moves to achieve our needs. We have to believe, and this is where focusing our work on expanding our consciousness will serve us well.

II

REPRIORITISE GOALS

I n *A Brief History of Humankind*, Yuval Noah Harari shares how Homo sapiens succeeded in being the dominant human race. It is my observation that because of this primal need to fight off other species, we still hold on to this need and mentality to dominate to survive when there are no other human species to compete with. Unknowingly, we are competing with ourselves and the very lifeforms that support and provide the ecosystem services we need to live, work, and play. We know Mother Earth's wrath well. It is no longer about safeguarding ourselves from rising temperatures with UV-protective fashion and air-conditioning.

It is about bringing *everything* we know back to *balance*.

Everything is interconnected. $E=mc^2$, an equation formulated by Albert Einstein, demonstrates that a small amount of mass can be transformed into a significant amount of energy.[10] This innate understanding of how we may efficiently convert our resources to reduce our dependence on non-renewable resources and minimise waste can promote more sustainable management of air, water, soil, energy, and metals. We will also require

---

[10] Perkowitz, S., Britannica, *E=mc²*, *September 9 2024*, https://www.britannica. com/science/E-mc2-equation (Accessed 11 September 2024).

many localised thriving ecosystems for co-prosperity to be realised. It cannot ensue with the persistent one-dimensional pursuit of economic gains through monopolisation and centralisation of power. Many ground-up initiatives are not seeing the light of day compared to these big businesses. Widespread standardisation of services and products to the extent that it wipes out diversification due to its underlying homogeneity is not natural. It is also not sustainable. Very few of these businesses boast sustainability wins as they do profit margins. Most of their products lack the product or service ingenuity to transition to circular economy approaches, compared to startups, for example, who are ensuring remanufacturing and servitisation are part of their business model.

On the other hand, financiers argue that many emerging business solutions lack financial viability because they are often still in the Research and Development stage, lack commercial value, or cannot scale to meet specific market conditions. If we wait for these solutions to demonstrate shorter payback periods and guarantee immediate revenue or profit, we risk ignoring the long-term impacts of climate change on future generations. Money circulating in the hands of a few needs to flow out to balance the hunger, starvation and deprivation of many worldwide. The Truth is that none of us are thrilled when someone suffers. Good news – the end of suffering is possible when we return to nature. Therefore, this book invites us to revisit how we show up to ourselves, others and Mother Earth. Feel the stagnant waters within us, manifesting as aches/pains/blocks to the movement we truly want to make.

Here are some reflection prompts to help us gain a deeper understanding of our current state and identify areas for growth and optimisation across various dimensions of our lives:

Physical Well-being

1. **Physical Flow:**
   How do I feel physically today?

   Are there any areas of tension or discomfort? What steps can I take to address them?

   _____

   _____

2. **Activity and Rest:**
   What balance am I maintaining between physical activity and rest?

   _____

   _____

   How does this impact my overall well-being?

   _____

   _____

3. **Feedback awareness:**
   Are there comments or observations people have shared about my energy levels or how I present myself? Do I agree?

   _____

   _____

   What information am I privy to about my family's health conditions, and what preventive steps am I taking to mitigate these issues from surfacing/flaring up?

   _____

   _____

Mental Health

1. **Thought Patterns:**
   What recurring thoughts or mental patterns are influencing me right now?

   _____

   _____

   Are these thoughts serving me positively or negatively?

   _____

   _____

2. **Knowledge Intake:**
   What types of information have I been consuming?

   _____

   _____

   How does this information contribute to my mental clarity and stimulation?

   _____

   _____

3. **Feedback awareness:**
   Have people commented or observed how I have been responding to situations?

   _____

   _____

   Am I aware of the language or vocabulary I am using? As well as how I speak to others. Is there a difference between how I talk to strangers and loved ones? If so, why is there a difference? (*Please note that there is more value in being curious than judgmental. We all have quirks, which means we must work through certain unresolved traumas.*)

   _____

   _____

Emotional Well-being

1. **Emotional State:**
   What emotions have I been experiencing regularly recently? Are they very different or consistent? How do these emotions make me feel?

   _____

   _____

   How do these emotions affect my daily interactions and decision-making? What mood am I generally in, and how does this impact people around me?

   _____

   _____

2. **Emotional Management:**
   How do I currently manage stress or emotional challenges?

   _____

   _____

   Are there additional strategies I could implement to improve my emotional resilience, especially in situations outside my control?

   _____

   _____

3. **Feedback awareness:**
   Have people commented or observed how I have been responding to situations?

   _____

   _____

   What do I notice about people's responses to my emotional sharing or feedback about challenging situations? How can this be improved?

   _____

   _____

Spiritual Connection

1. **Innate Gift:**
   How connected do I feel to my inner world and my sense of purpose in life?

   _____

   _____

   Are there any practices that help me strengthen this important connection?

   _____

   _____

2. **Natural Emergence:**
   What desires or passions have surfaced within me recently that make me smile?

   _____

   _____

   How can I nurture and express these natural inclinations in my daily life without making drastic changes?

   _____

   _____

3. **Feedback from others:**
   Have people made comments or observations about my presence? Do they notice any shifts in my temperament due to my spiritual practices?

   _____

   _____

   Am I aware of how I present myself to avoid coming across as self-righteous? How am I forgiving towards others who may not understand my beliefs?

   _____

   _____

Inter-relational Quotient

1. **Relationship Quality:**
   How would I describe the quality of my current relationships? What steps can I take to enhance these connections further?

   _____

   _____

   Are there learned unhealthy behaviours or mindsets towards people concerning trust that I may have internalised from my caregivers?

   _____

   _____

2. **Communication Skills:**
   How effectively do I communicate with others regarding challenging emotions or issues? Are there areas where I can improve to foster better understanding and connection?

   _____

   _____

Community Engagement

1. **Community Impact:**
   How involved am I in my community?

   _____

   _____

   What are some ways I could contribute more meaningfully to the collective well-being of this group or others? Perhaps through donating resources or raising awareness of their initiatives?

   _____

   _____

2. Shared Purpose:

How aligned do I feel with the goals and values of the community I am part of? (*Please note that our community engagements need to be equally energising for us as they are for those who receive our support. If, for some reason, we feel drained, we need to reflect on the situation to ensure we are optimising our time and energy to contribute in a way that enriches us, too.*)

_____

_____

How can I strengthen this inner alignment and support the community's growth?

_____

_____

If we allow it, our hearts and emotions can guide us toward co-prospering with others. Many struggle to accept, feel, and process difficult emotions, but it is never too late to begin reparenting ourselves. We unlock our innate creativity by showing our inner child that they are safe to express their true nature, which is childlike, fun, and playful. Contrary to the belief that we must suppress our inner child to fulfil adult responsibilities, we can embrace both. Even at seventy, we can joyfully co-create our lives with our inner child. The key lies in maturity. Much like wisdom, maturity enables us to communicate clearly and thoughtfully, preventing us from causing harm to others. It allows us to engage fully in life, even when faced with challenges. It manifests through awareness of our thoughts, feelings and actions. Through every life experience, we can cultivate a greater maturity that empowers us to love life and maintain our playfulness while living responsibly.

When we live consciously with nature, we develop a profound love for our planet. We become aware of her suffering and take meaningful steps to make a difference, knowing that every small action counts. Each ounce of dignity matters as our hearts sync with her rhythm. In this interconnectedness, we find a true sense of home within ourselves, prompting us to take actions that positively impact the Earth. With compassion, we recognise that others may not yet share this experience, and we can hold space and hope for their journey toward inner harmony with nature. This awareness extends to the spaces we inhabit as energy flows within us and into our environments. Prioritising the greening of our buildings has become increasingly essential in recent years. Sustainable building design addresses important issues such as mitigating climate change and improving indoor thermal comfort, ensuring both occupant well-being and the property's longevity—a win-win for developers and renters alike.

However, there is more we can do. We can choose eco-friendly materials, minimise demolition, and focus on refurbishing and retrofitting existing structures. It is also crucial for consumers to consider the implications of their choices when opting for brand-new homes. We need to engage in conversations about what truly benefits our communities. Do we want to continue facing air, water, and soil pollution from constantly constructing new buildings?

By aligning our practices with nature, we create a more sustainable future for ourselves and the planet.

We must rethink our priorities to move forward effectively, focusing on what truly matters despite the trade-offs. Any small shift counts. Nature offers valuable lessons on how to share knowledge and maintain a healthy ecosystem. It follows natural cycles, showing us when and how change happens. For example, we see how plants and animals change with the seasons, from winter to spring to summer and autumn. By studying these natural systems, we can better manage our operations. Nature knows when to let go of what is not working. It easily creates as it destroys. Similarly, we can be more willing to step back from specific outcomes to create a balanced approach that aligns with the more significant flow of life around us. This includes considering what would make our lives more straightforward and enriching.

We truly understand sustainability when we commit to never abandoning or harming ourselves again. When we recognise that we are enough, we understand ourselves holistically. Our ability to be here right now stems from faith and trust that creative intelligence will guide us to our destination. Present-moment consciousness can help us let go and allow ourselves to be led from within, even if this opposes mainstream ways of being. What deep fear emerges when we submit to this process? It is often this unsettling question about our attitude towards ourselves when we have 'nothing' – to do, have or be.

If we can come to terms with this state of being 'nothing': love it as it is, accept it as it is and know this is not the be-all and end-all, we can transcend all depths of fear around surrendering. We can begin to flow with the universe instead of against it and be sure to realise our hidden talents as we embark on this journey. We each came to be our unique selves because we have something special to offer. Let us begin to unravel that. In this process, we must keep our eye on the North Star by avoiding extremes and staying focused on achieving balance in everything we do and whomever we are with.

We frequently ask ourselves, "What is needed for my highest evolutionary growth that will also support everyone around me?"[11]

If you often find yourself doing everything for others, it may not be helpful; in fact, it can lead to feelings of resentment, regardless of how self-sacrificial or loving your intentions may be. Conversely, taking time for your healing is not selfish. Investing in yourself brings benefits that go far beyond what we might expect. As we grow our consciousness and

---

[11] *Please note any question or prompt in this book is not meant for us to take drastic actions to change our lives or uproot what makes us feel safe and secure. If we feel called to do so at any point, it will be helpful to sit on the decision for 24 hours and notice the emotions instead. Our sense of anguish or pain could be more deep-seated than the situation at hand, and we may simply be repeating patterns from our past or active ancestral imprints, which can be more harmful than we think. Hence, by practising our discretion to ensure we are not emotionally reacting, we can be more aware of what is important for our well-being. Here, prudence will be equally valuable. This is the ability to govern and discipline ourselves using reason, skill, and sound judgment when considering our resources.*

awareness, we become better equipped to hold space for others going through their process. Unconditional love is empowerment. It recognises our humanity and makes inroads to strengthen our connection with ourselves. It is healthy boundaries where we are realistic and grounded in our approach to what is self-sustainable despite big hopes and visions of what we wish to achieve. It is self-respect where we are mindful of our own needs, emotions, and values to ensure they are upheld so that we can practice and live by them. Dignity ensures we know we are all worthy of forgiveness and reconciliation, especially with ourselves, no matter how we have been treated.

A distinction must be made between stability and an intricate balance in life. Equilibrium is finding the middle ground in everything to help us stay balanced. Max Planck, a renowned physicist, proposed that all matter is sustained by a force that orchestrates the vibrations of atoms, implying the existence of a conscious and intelligent mind behind it.[12] This perspective highlights the significance of awareness in navigating entropy, which is crucial for regulators and corporations to grasp. We are in the pilot seat, and Figure 4 shows the different layers of human perception that can impact our level of awareness and, therefore, our response or reaction to crises, both known and unknown.

---

[12]   S. Borowski, American Association for the Advancement of Science (AAAS), 'Quantum mechanics and the consciousness connection', 16 July 2012, https://www.aaas.org/taxonomy/term/10/quantum-mechanics-and-consciousness-connection (Accessed 31 May 2024).

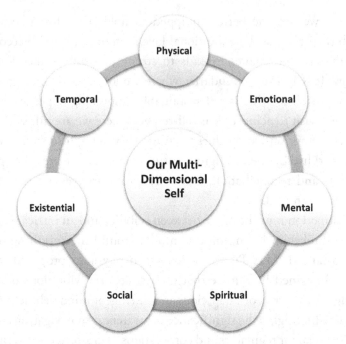

Figure 4: The many aspects that inform our consciousness at a single point in time

Our communications, driven by the hyper-masculine environments in which we operate, disconnect us from our intuition that can help us discern what is not known to us and make choices that align with a higher good. This requires ego-deaths for most of us to acknowledge that we are better off operating from our heart space than our minds. When we make quantum shifts in how we relate to one another and understand body language and emotional expressions, we can understand that our mental thinking models for strategies and roadmaps are insufficient. How we may bring the end user or stakeholder along with us on a journey they can relate to often requires an appeal to our emotions. We know this when we catch a certain Ad or movie that thugs on our heartstrings. The question is, how have we become so disconnected from this innate knowing? And how may we connect with our existential purpose for being here right now, in our roles in our lives?

Figure 5 details the underlying dynamics of interpersonal communications, which can affect how we perceive and relate to each other.

If unaware, we might be seeding further discord and misunderstanding through our behaviours stemming from the unknown mechanisms running our beliefs and mindsets. We can uncover these now with the many tools offered in the marketplace to unpack how we contribute to our realities. Mindfulness is one simple practice we can implement immediately to activate our awareness muscle and strengthen it with consistent practice.

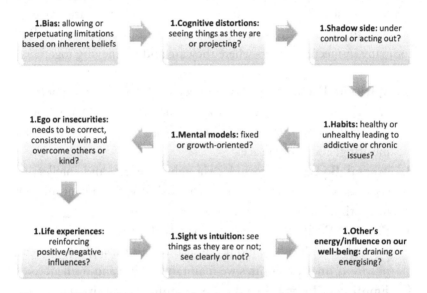

Figure 5: If we reference the iceberg analogy – these aspects would form the submerged complexities to be uncovered in any given situation

In addition, we are often plagued by different time horizons that require us to unpack our brittle, anxious, non-linear, and incomprehensible (BANI) world by responding to it as it is. Realising the future is not predetermined will be key. It comprises various potential outcomes based on the actions we are taking right now. Therefore, when charting our organisational or personal transformation roadmaps, we can be mindful of the different types of outcomes possible based on our investment of resources. It is essential to align with the broader market goals through research and partnerships focused on knowledge sharing and peer-to-peer learning. This approach allows us to co-create strategies that align with collective changes, minimising resistance during implementation. The emphasis is increasing awareness of decarbonisation, low-carbon alternatives, and circular economy opportunities.[13] These insights help businesses train and redesign processes to meet emerging compliance and industry standards. More importantly, they help future-proof organisations, fostering trust with stakeholders.

Organisations and individuals can positively shape tomorrow's outcomes by taking responsibility for their actions today. This is where we may embrace wholeness with our Sustainability Inside-Out™ framework, shown in Figure 6. As co-creators in this vast universe, we exist together with others. As we unpack our journeys, we find company in meeting others where they are and journeying together.

1. **Spiritual Dimension:** This aspect connects us to something greater—the transcendent, the divine, or our inner wisdom. Nurturing our spiritual well-being helps us discover purpose, meaning, and inner peace.

2. **Mental Body:** This includes thoughts, beliefs, and intellectual pursuits. Cultivating mental clarity, curiosity, and a commitment to continuous learning enhances our well-being.

3. **Physical Body:** Our physical body is the vessel that carries us through life. Prioritising our physical health through movement, nutrition, and rest ensures we maintain vitality and resilience.

4. **Emotional Body:** Often the most familiar yet elusive dimension, our emotional body encompasses our feelings, empathy, and emotional intelligence. Understanding and nurturing this aspect is crucial for a balanced life.

5. **Inter-relational:** By building authentic bonds, practising empathy, and fostering compassion, we form relationships that enrich our lives.

6. **Community:** A community reflects our shared context—the broader social fabric that impacts how we think, feel, and act. Contributing positively to our local or global communities gives us a sense of purpose and promotes collective well-being, which cannot be understated.

---

[13]   Lacy P., Spindler W., Long J., World Economic Forum, *How Can Businesses Accelerate The Transition To A Circular Economy*, 20 January 2020, https://www.weforum.org/agenda/2020/01/how-can-we-accelerate-the-transition-to-a-circular-economy/.

Figure 6: The Sustainability Inside-Out™
encapsulating our multi-dimensional Self

Neglecting any of these facets usually creates an imbalance. By consistently self-reflecting to adjust our intention and attention, we can maintain a holistic outlook on life within ourselves and our interactions with others. This practice can help us better understand our daily emotions by identifying the connecting themes across different aspects of our lives. To begin, take a piece of paper or a notebook and draw six overlapping circles. The centre, where all the circles intersect, will be filled in later as we input our experiences into the respective circles. By charting fear- and love-based experiences, we can uncover more about our shadow side—the parts of our personality that we may have suppressed or repressed over time. This comprehensive framework also enables us to track our progress toward our goals.

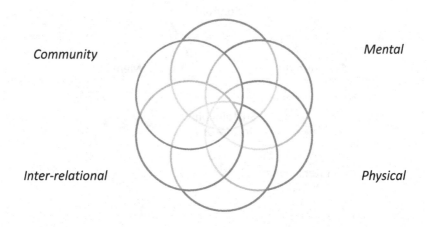

Spiritual

Community

Mental

Inter-relational

Physical

Emotional

Figure 7: How to implement the Sustainability Inside-Out™ framework

To unpack difficult emotions, consider the following prompts:

- What is happening, and how do I feel about it?
- How does this situation affect me?
- What beliefs are being challenged or surfaced that I need to address?
- How can I safely release negative emotions or feel better?
- Have I reached a moment of clarity or breakthrough?
- What am I grateful for?
- Who supports me in this journey?
- What motivates me? What is my 'why'?
- How can I truly let go? What is holding me back?
- What is the worst that could happen if I let go?
- What actions do I need to take to flourish and grow?
- Is there someone or something I perceive as controlling me?
- What challenges am I facing? What obstacles appear in my path, and how can I reframe them?

A breakthrough is likely as we practice self-care, self-love and self-compassion because we fundamentally accept our true nature as a loving, happy and peaceful soul. Anything that takes us away from this reality is not out to attack, harm or disturb us. Rather, it is to show us that acceptance comes with wisdom, knowing that nothing is perfect and that all experiences have a purpose: to bring us back in alignment with ourselves.

The Zero-Point Practice: *Neutralising Inner Conflict*

In the practice of zero-point meditation, we explore a waking life modality. As we navigate our day, interacting with various people, we consciously and unconsciously experience life. This practice centres around allowing perceived negative and positive events to occur while counterbalancing them with their opposing force. When we perceive a situation as negative, looking for its silver lining is important to help neutralise that negativity just as much as uncovering the root source of this pain. Similarly, in positive experiences, we should remain grounded by acknowledging our dualistic nature and tendencies. This practice helps us achieve a state of equilibrium and non-judgment, which can significantly improve our mental well-being by reducing our reactions and expectations. We become less affected by external circumstances because we understand that people and situations are often not what they seem. There are always two sides to every coin.

The zero-point practice helps us commit to purification by self-correcting how our emotions and thought patterns respond to what life presents us daily. This ensures we are as self-aware as possible of not just negative but also of the positive moments. When we reflect, we may also go through the day backwards, starting from the most recent memory since it is still fresh in our minds and charting the various points in the day where our well-being was either shaken or bolstered thanks to our thoughts, actions and words spoken. Knowing this helps us align and stick to our desired habits and achieve the goals we want in our lives.

As we chart this daily, we can start noticing patterns and trends, which may lead us to further contemplations and moments of epiphanies. This self-investment pays in the long term as it helps us evolve and expand our awareness of how we perceive, respond and react to life. It also aids in cultivating an attitude of gratitude. The more grateful we are for both the 'good' and 'bad' stuff, the less controlling we get about certain outcomes we may think we 'deserve'. We know nothing is personal. We suspend judgment and hold our inner peace for longer periods each time, which reduces our stress levels and raises our vibration!

Understanding triggers and recognising their value is crucial for our healing journey. The real transformation occurs in how we respond when we are triggered. Do we take the time to sit with ourselves, approaching the situation with curiosity, like a concerned friend or therapist would? We must cultivate this practice with ourselves to reclaim our power and promote our well-being. Triggers can serve as external prompts that encourage us to feel emotions we may have suppressed. Many of us experience numbness and uncertainty when feelings arise, leading us to brush them aside instinctively. However, what if there is power to experience these emotions fully? Triggers—from a familiar smell, sight, or sound—can bring unresolved issues from our inner world to the surface. Facing these issues allows us to let go and free ourselves from the pain or misleading beliefs we have internalised over time. These beliefs often stem from accumulated thought processes and reinforced unhelpful patterns.

To navigate our triggers effectively, we should employ logical and objective questioning techniques that suspend self-judgment and foster self-acceptance. This approach helps us remain trigger-free and promotes emotional resilience. Take a moment to acknowledge the feeling that has arisen. Instead of pushing it away, allow yourself to be present with the emotion. Mindfulness research suggests that observing our feelings without immediate reaction can reduce their intensity and help us gain clarity. Rather than avoiding discomfort, embrace it as a natural part of the emotional experience. Studies show that sitting with discomfort can lead to greater emotional intelligence and resilience. Recognising discomfort allows us to understand it better. Instead of resisting the feeling, lean into it. Explore where the sensation manifests in your body. Body awareness techniques, such as those used in somatic therapy, highlight that our emotions often have physical counterparts. By connecting with these sensations, we can process emotions more deeply.

Treat yourself with the kindness and compassion you would offer a distressed child. This self-soothing technique creates a sense of safety and acceptance, which can help you access more profound insights. Self-compassion practices, supported by research from Dr. Kristin Neff[14], show that self-kindness can significantly improve emotional well-being and reduce anxiety. Allow time for the feelings to unfold without rushing to resolve them. Patience is key to understanding the underlying causes of our triggers. Reflective practices like journaling or meditation can help us wait for insights to emerge organically, fostering a deeper understanding of our emotional landscape.

By following these steps, we can cultivate a more profound understanding of ourselves, reduce the impact of triggers, and enhance our emotional well-being. This process fosters personal growth and strengthens our ability to navigate life's challenges easily. Just like triggers, understanding our cravings can also be beneficial. When you reach for that bag of chips or comfort food—especially if it's on your "avoid" list—recognise that a significant insight is trying to surface, even if you are inclined to ignore or avoid it. We often crave the crunch of food to drown out inner chaos, seeking to self-soothe and comfort ourselves with a familiar distraction.

Breaking this habit with some reflection could help clarify reasons that may not be immediately clear. These cravings or reaching out to other forms of reassurance signal that we do not feel comfortable or safe. It is a signal for us to take note that something is bothering us. It is also a sign that we are not feeding our bodies what we need to avoid these physical cravings in the first place. Something profound is emerging to be witnessed within us, and if we allow it to move up from our bellies to our hearts, we may know what it is. However, we usually suppress it with what we call 'comfort food', which may make us feel full, bloated or guilty – basically 'distracted' to address its real cause. This is because the origin emotion is a fear we are unwilling to face and accept.

---

14   Find out more about Dr Kristin Neff's work here: https://self-compassion.org/

We may think addressing the issue might make us spiral out or fall into a low mood, and we have to be happy and put together, right? We must shift away from this line of thinking as it is to our detriment in the long haul. Our emotions are not bad because they are a part of us. They help us understand life and what aligns with our hearts. When we lead more and more from our heart space, we will understand this power, and we will not be fearful of our emotions again. Instead, it sets us free like never before. Our unhelpful habits do not hold us back; we dare to learn more about ourselves by sitting with what wants to meet us.

What if the easiest and most health-effective way to do this was to tell ourselves, 'Please reveal your truth to my pain; I want to know,' and then wait? Wait for the pain to show where it is in the physical body, where it resides in the emotional body, and what thoughts/visions are emerging in the mental body.

Does this emotion uplift or dampen our spirit, and how are we being with people around us?

Bad moods and poor social regulation usually reflect underlying pain that wants to express itself but is unsure how. The more we suppress it, the more disconnected we may feel. *Am I also putting myself down when I speak of myself?*

These are all signs of reaching our limits and needing to turn *inward* to heal.

The realisations that come through from addressing our inner pain may be painful on all fronts, and this is primarily to snap us out of our delusion or illusion state to start seeing things as they are, which is usually not as great as we tell ourselves (and we do this so that we can cope). And it is ok to grieve our circumstances – how did we get here; how did we not know better, and how will we get out? Many times, it is old pain buried deep within us that we may have unconsciously repressed or consciously suppressed to avoid or deflect feeling it. This discomfort has occurred in our earlier history or timelines as a soul. How we choose to heal or resolve it comes with simple awareness, observing what we do when this comes up and reflecting to decide how we want to address/overcome it. If we are placing our attention onto something else instead, this is either a distraction or a deflection of our problems.

And if a situation occurs externally to your loved ones, perhaps, and is triggering you, ask yourself: *Why does this affect me? What is the theme here, and has this happened before?*

How am I going to feel better about it?

Have I accepted the problem's dualistic nature—that it is both a pain and a blessing? What is the silver lining or lesson waiting to unfold once I address my initial emotions?

Reprioritising our goals requires rebalancing our multi-dimensional state. This means we are bringing everything back to focus by adjusting the lenses that govern how we perceive and realise what is happening around us. Going through this passage requires self-compassion, forgiveness and bravery because it will differ for each of us. Facing this upheaval within usually follows a release, which hugely benefits cleansing our systems to be more online with our soul. We will feel better after we process the density of any emotions that want to be cleared. Choose to *reframe* whenever a difficult or unknown emotion wants to express itself within us.

Our job is to meet ourselves where we can and make amends. We deserve to be there for ourselves.

We must remind ourselves that taking responsibility for how we feel, think, and act will help us feel lighter now. We must also remind ourselves that our soul origin is peaceful, happy, and loving. Any deviation from these core states of being is our way of returning to safety, protection, and home within us. With this thinking process, we are undeterred from facing what is 'hidden' within us to heal and course-correct towards what will always serve our highest good: love and limitless potential. Through this process, we inherently gain dignity consciousness because we realise our self-worth and that of others.

How do we see ourselves when no one is looking?

How do we describe ourselves when curating an online profile, and is this how we see ourselves?

Is there a difference between these versions, and how may we bridge the authenticity gap? What are we willing to reveal about ourselves that will help others understand and relate to us better?

When we heal, we manifest our best potential by focusing on what serves the highest good for ourselves and others.

No one else can walk this journey, for us. When we commit, we liberate the cycles of fear, constriction, and holding ourselves back commonly experienced in our families and societies. Freedom is more accessible, and we appreciate everything that has brought us to this pivotal realisation. There is no more confusion, doubt, or blaming. We are flowing with creative intelligence, which positively impacts the trajectories of those around us. Inspiration uplifts all of us once we begin.

Duality is commonplace in our interactions with others. When reconciling our shadow side, we step more into the light because of greater self-awareness. We can also assess fear-based programming and change it to loving kindness for ourselves and others. This practice gets easier when we engage more with our intuitive selves daily by checking how balanced we feel in our well-being quotients.

Therefore, success in achieving overall well-being is when we seek to create happiness while extending the benefit of the doubt to others. This is different from avoidance or denial. We are called to acknowledge the situation and people as they are and to make choices that uphold our inner harmony, which naturally translates to outward peace. Reprioritising goals requires us to understand the multidimensional realities we each bring to our relationships—at the workplace or home. Hence, managing our strategic foresight exercises to shift our cognitive, emotional, and behavioural patterns from avoidance to engagement is more important than striving for the results of *a* vision. In a BANI world—brittle, anxious, non-linear, and incomprehensible—we must truly challenge our perceptions of the realities we live in and collaborate to create more rewarding and supportive outcomes with one another. The best plans are no plans that birth innovation out of a necessity to evolve.

How, then, do we manifest our preferred futures?

When we fail to address challenging situations, we often select a reality that fits our existing narrative, leading to confusion, especially if others see things differently. Cultural backgrounds and social conditioning can contribute to the spread of toxicity when we cannot clarify misunderstandings and feel pressured to appease others or conform. As a result, many of us opt for avoidance, as it seems less complicated and more manageable. In contrast, some of us exaggerate our feelings to ensure we are heard. This requires more energy, which can quickly lead to burnout. Others minimise their experiences to create a false sense of hope, which could be more harmful than avoidance in the first place. When we avoid something, we remain silent, which does not necessarily mean we are better off than those who react by exaggerating or minimising their feelings. Silence can indicate a more profound detachment from reality as a coping mechanism. We may struggle to understand or ignore what is happening out of fear or apathy.

The impact of these behaviours is further exacerbated when we believe we are in control.

Indeed, we can control our choices, actions, thoughts, and behaviours at any given moment, but not the outcomes, how others will think, act, or feel, nor the unforeseen events that may arise. At this juncture, the collective has become too accustomed to our established habits, where thoughts and emotions are predominantly negative, fuelled by worry. These often involve envisioning the worst possible outcomes, anticipated threats, or challenging situations. Such patterns reflect our internal state more than our actual reality. To perceive with clarity and make discerning judgments, suspending unfounded fears and maintaining an acute awareness of our five senses as we engage in work, leisure, and life across various environments is essential. We can hold out a vision for a better tomorrow and do our best to work towards it by flowing and being transparent like water. We are neither stressed nor controlling the situation, but we are choosing to be present and mindful of the evolving state of affairs to take the next best course of action with as much awareness as possible.

Reprioritising for a sustainable future requires us to be anchored in the present moment, which allows us to maintain awareness of our well-being and emotional safety. From this place of inner peace, we gain the freedom to respond thoughtfully to our circumstances rather than simply reacting. Equally important is the well-being of our organisations. By understanding our "why," we can explore the "how." Employing simulations to create a digital twin can be invaluable for larger organisations, particularly those with multiple locations and diverse business needs. This technology helps monitor an organisation's health and identify discrepancies in management, enabling proactive solutions to unhealthy work environments.

As we navigate a rapidly changing landscape, strategic insights through integrity-enhancing platforms become essential. These tools allow us to manage business risks, adapt to market changes, and address legal compliance issues. We must also consider the consequences of mergers, acquisitions, and layoffs, all of which contribute to uncertainty and shape our future outcomes. To create a cohesive and nature-positive future, we must embrace the concept of 'harmony'. This means recognising that we no longer need to compete for survival; instead, we can focus on collaboration. By understanding that we each bring unique value, we can work together to find complementary solutions, ensuring no one is left behind.

Awareness is the starting point for this transformation. It helps us recognise areas needing attention and prevents unconscious impulses from leading to chaos, especially in time management, financial decisions, and emotional well-being. By prioritising emotional stability over ego-driven actions, we can build high-performing teams and foster innovation. As we move forward, technology must shift from serving defensive or extractive purposes to fostering connection, healing, and creativity. It should bridge divides and emphasise our collective potential, focusing on scalable and accessible opportunities for everyone, especially those in eco-spiritual environments. This requires moving away from technology that maintains surface-level connections to one that enriches our personal and collective experiences.

We must transition from fast consumerism to a more thoughtful use of technology that enhances our spiritual and emotional lives. Effective governance will play a crucial role in maintaining the integrity of our systems, moving beyond reactive legal frameworks to proactive, integrity-focused cultures. This involves implementing sound regulations, supporting high-quality research, and providing guidance for the responsible use of technologies like AI. Harnessing collective intelligence through participatory processes can enhance decision-making in complex systems. Organisations can tap into collective wisdom for meaningful impact by improving meeting effectiveness and visualising discussions.

However, we must also address the challenges of increased connectivity and boundary-less systems. Trust, ethical conduct, and responsible consumption will become paramount, necessitating a new social contract that protects privacy and aligns with contemporary values. As we pursue a more trustworthy future through technology, we embrace awareness, responsible practices, collaboration, and effective governance. These principles are essential for navigating complexity and driving sustainable innovation, particularly in traditional sectors like regulatory and corporate environments. Achieving these goals will require playful experimentation, continuous improvement, and self-awareness of our limitations. Upholding boundaries is crucial, as is fostering an ethical mindset that allows trust-enhancing technology to flourish. A certain level of follow-through on our intended theories of change needs to occur at a massive scale now (an example of a corporate sustainability initiative's theory of change is exemplified in Table 2).

Internal goals →	What we publicly disclose →	True value created →	Outcomes received →	Outcomes desired →	Action fulfilled
Reduce waste Sustainability business mindset	Actions taken Achievement made	EGSEE-related score results	Carbon emissions avoided Trust created Innovation generated	Net zero 2050 Carbon neutrality Halving biodiversity loss by 2030 Transitioning to circular economic practices	In-depth understanding **Relevant and robust knowledge** of all the ecosystem players and their moving parts **Strong ethics** to think for the whole even when tackling one organisational change or leadership improvement

Table 2: a high-level breakdown of how corporations understand their responsibility to act, which can be easily emulated in other stakeholder groups as well

Ultimately, technology must be based on unbiased algorithms promoting equitable partnerships and fair access. It must transcend outdated beliefs about power and corruption, uniting us to solve problems efficiently and with a long-term perspective. For future-proofing public policy, we need an integrated approach incorporating disaster risk mitigation, climate adaptation through nature-based solutions, and advanced waste management to embed circularity across value chains. The current linear economy mindset must shift to prioritise reuse, reconditioning, and recycling, particularly in public procurement practices. By taking grounded actions now, we can influence positive change in ourselves and others. Change takes time, but we must formulate strategies that align with the evolving world to avoid chaos in our internal and external systems.

Let us return to our roots and reconnect with the natural world.

In this chapter, we have gained valuable insights into how we may reprioritise our goals, drawing from a species that has thrived throughout history with its unique and striking features. Historically, peacocks have been admired for their beauty and have been symbols of renewal and divinity in various cultures. Their magnificent feathers, adorned with eye-like patterns, are often associated with prosperity and good luck, reflecting transformation and change. By connecting with the peacock, we can appreciate its deep blue hues, which remind us of nature's vibrancy. This connection helps us gain clarity and perspective, allowing us to see beyond surface appearances and understand situations more deeply. It also emphasises our relationship with the natural world, from which we can always draw inspiration and insight. Equally important is our life force energy, sustained by energy sources surrounding us. What we nourish ourselves with, watch and stimulate matters. Ensuring we can always stay centred and balanced would be vital to knowing when to reprioritise existing goals to support our healing journeys back to ourselves.

III

REFOCUS ATTENTION

The Atlantic Council's Freedom and Prosperity Center has developed two significant indexes: the Freedom and Prosperity Index. These tools assess the levels of liberty and economic well-being across 164 countries.[15] According to a multi-year analysis in its 2024 report, prosperity has grown across all regions compared to 2012, even with the impact of the COVID-19 pandemic.[16] However, developing countries

---

[15] I. Campomanes; N. Dannaoui; J. Lemoine; D. Negrea, 'The Path to Prosperity: The 2024 Freedom and Prosperity Indexes', Atlantic Council, June 25 2024, https://www.atlanticcouncil.org/in-depth-research-reports/report/the-path-to-prosperity-the-2024-freedom-and-prosperity-indexes/ (Accessed 11 September 2024); Each index scores countries on a scale from 0 to 100, with higher scores indicating greater freedom or prosperity. The Freedom Index assesses economic, political, and legal freedoms, categorizing countries into "free," "mostly free," "mostly unfree," or "unfree" based on their scores. Meanwhile, the Prosperity Index evaluates income, health, education, environment, minority rights, and inequality, placing countries into "prosperous," "mostly prosperous," "mostly unprosperous," or "unprosperous" categories. The indexes cover data from 1995 to 2022. For the most recent updates, the Freedom Index primarily uses 2022 data, while the Prosperity Index relies on 2021 data, filling in gaps with earlier data if needed. Please read page 27 for more details on the 'Methodology'.

[16] Campomanes, Dannaoui, Lemoine and Negrea, 'The Path to Prosperity: The 2024 Freedom and Prosperity Indexes', p.18.

have not been able to progress quicker than wealthy countries since 2013, compared to the previous decade.[17] Further, while there is a proven correlation between freedom and prosperity where 'freer countries are more prosperous', minority rights have consistently declined since 2013 due to a weak political environment and institutions.[18]

'The sustained increase in the global prosperity score halted in 2020 due to the effects of the COVID-19 pandemic and still lags the 2019 level'.[19]

Our intergovernmental systems worldwide have made progress toward promoting shared prosperity. In 2020, the World Economic Forum and its partners highlighted that effective governance must serve as the foundation for achieving goals related to the planet, people, and prosperity (see Table 3).[20] Still, current structures designed to manage our planet's and human systems' complex and dynamic nature pose challenges. We need greater flexibility, interconnectivity, and transparent real-time information flow to build trust within these systems.

[17]   Campomanes, Dannaoui, Lemoine and Negrea, 'The Path to Prosperity: The 2024 Freedom and Prosperity Indexes', p.1.

[18]   Campomanes, Dannaoui, Lemoine and Negrea, 'The Path to Prosperity: The 2024 Freedom and Prosperity Indexes', p.22.

[19]   Campomanes, Dannaoui, Lemoine and Negrea, 'The Path to Prosperity: The 2024 Freedom and Prosperity Indexes', p.18.

[20]   World Economic Forum, Measuring Stakeholder Capitalism Towards Common Metrics and Consistent Reporting of Sustainable Value Creation, Whitepaper, September 2020.

PRINCIPLES OF GOVERNANCE	PLANET	PEOPLE	PROSPERITY
THE DEFINITION OF GOVERNANCE IS EVOLVING AS ORGANISATIONS ARE INCREASINGLY EXPECTED TO DEFINE AND EMBED THEIR PURPOSE AT THE CENTRE OF THEIR BUSINESS. BUT THE PRINCIPLES OF AGENCY, ACCOUNTABILITY AND STEWARDSHIP REMAIN VITAL FOR TRULY "GOOD" GOVERNANCE.	An ambition is to protect the planet from degradation, including through sustainable consumption and production, sustainably managing its natural resources and taking urgent action on climate change, so that it can support the needs of the present and future generations.	An ambition to end poverty and hunger, in all their forms and dimensions, and to ensure that all human beings can fulfil their potential in dignity and equality and in a healthy environment.	An ambition is to ensure that all human beings can enjoy prosperous and fulfilling lives and that economic, social and technological progress occurs in harmony with nature.

Table 3: recreated from the World Economic Forum's Whitepaper on Measuring Stakeholder Capitalism Towards Common Metrics and Consistent Reporting of Sustainable Value Creation

Spider energy embodies the connections and resilience we need. Just as a spider weaves a complex web larger than itself, we must take bold steps beyond our comfort zones, especially decision-makers. Staying in crisis mode can blind us to potential solutions. We must rally together and act on our intentions; the rest will follow. To create meaningful change, we must start at the individual level. Recognising our interconnectedness helps us understand how our thoughts, feelings, and actions shape our inner and outer worlds. This awareness can empower us to foster resilience that benefits our organisations and communities. We must also accept the legacy systems we currently navigate, even if they seem outdated. Our resilience can demonstrate new possibilities for value to decision-makers. We can gather support and drive progress toward our goals by forming partnerships and testing small initiatives.

As we transition to a New Earth, we must stay present, focusing on what is happening within and around us at every moment. Cultivating this awareness requires practice, often gained through years of spiritual training. In today's fast-paced world, quieting our minds amid the constant pull for instant gratification is challenging. However, being mindful of who we are and how we engage with others is essential. We must choose our words carefully, ensuring that our commitments are followed through with awareness of our limitations and opportunities. By building sustainably from the ground up, we can take measured steps forward to maintain momentum and achieve meaningful progress.

Recognising our interconnectedness and relationship with time and space can unravel the ties that bind us. This includes addressing karmic, cosmic, inter-relational, and intergenerational wounds that keep many of us trapped. Often, unseen influences—like empathic and telepathic connections—can steer us off our true path (refer to Chapter VI, Figure 16). Understanding how we function as energy beings is vital. We need to identify our optimal state versus our drained or fatigued state. Achieving this awareness requires daily practice and self-care, allowing us always to remain attuned to our inner world and physical state. This level of understanding goes beyond self-centeredness; it demands our commitment to embrace the repetitive nature of life, viewing it from different perspectives. With healing as our intention, we aim to align with our souls within our physical bodies. This alignment helps us stay connected to Truth, guided by our inner wisdom as we navigate life. We become more self-assured and recognise our unity with all that exists. There is no rush, separation, or divide in this space. There is also no absolute right or wrong.

We are simply aware of what is coming up to shift for all of us, *without* judgment.

Simple rules will include being mindful of any energetic leakages regarding indulgences, distractions or excessive thought/movement to avoid/neglect ourselves. 'Rest' takes on a new definition either in meditative state, rest state or contemplation. We avoid using tools like money to forgo our independence and freedom to take good care of ourselves. We avoid giving our powers away to ingest or hydrate ourselves with what eventually harms us. This includes environments and people. Instead, we bless these spaces and ensure we are upholding the integrity of our souls concerning what we are doing in each moment. Walking this path may sound challenging until it will not be. We will have to begin. When we eventually see the big picture of our respective ascension journeys, we will notice how we have been guided to use our free will for our highest good, despite what may have transpired. We are all evolving whether we know it or not, and we can accelerate this transformation pathway by being conscious. Change is inevitable, and given our transits, the likelihood of finance and financing changing is evident. With continued infrastructure damage, displacement of communities, and millions going into mitigation plans worldwide to safeguard our borders, there has to be an alternative to financing and refinancing for humanity's betterment.

We will require *new forms* of crisis management, crisis communications, risk acceptance and change management that *support rather than scare us into submission.*

Nature showcases this value well with 'mutualism' – where a tree gives refuge to a plant or insect only to receive its protection from predators or support in supplying nutrients to sustain its ecosystem. This helps us acknowledge the power of interdependence and how we build true value and competitive edges when we show up with our strengths for each other. The other is not a threat because we each offer unique contributions. For this to happen, we must always have true wealth internally. This is an unshakeable state of being that is undoubtedly contented with every blessing of an experience. For too long, as humanity, we have believed that being fiscally responsible means not going bankrupt, no matter what our money blueprint stories. We are so afraid of financial embarrassment that we would go to lengths, often against our values. However, what if this is where we have it all wrong? Who is defining this notion of fiscal responsibility?

It is not the system's fault; it is just a fault of the system design.

How, then, may we rethink fiscal responsibility in a way that aligns us with Mother Earth and the sustainability of our future generations? Is monetary wealth the only denominator here?

We cannot solve New World problems with constant outsourcing at the expense of others and pursuing existing financing methods, specifically concerning debt financing. If we look at the global situation, debt in emerging markets or lower-privileged demographics impedes our overall societal growth. Our current systemic and historical baggage has benefitted some and kept others locked into cycles they are either aware or unaware of. The few who make it out try their best to keep moving forward, and we are constantly reminded of this dynamic regardless of how far we go — like survivors' guilt. There is, therefore, a need to think of bolder, more intuitive, and more grounded solutions that can uplift the whole.

We need new value creation regarding money as an asset class.

The good news is we have individual data sets and publicly available databases churning invaluable insights in their realms. Banks with digital infrastructures have real-time access to end users' spending, saving and loan default possibilities. We have to bridge this information using stable, secure, and super-fast technologies like quantum computing to build a securitised interface of interlocking information streams that promote the transboundary flow of information to reimagine fiscal responsibility for all. Current commodities must extend to supporting human ingenuity instead of scalable platform ideas that already exist. We need to start thinking beyond fiscal/monetary terms. Time banking and sharing economies are examples of how we may re-introduce bartering to help turn the social safety nets of our societies into floors. How we may incentivise our people beyond handouts to create more purpose-fit jobs and social resiliency across our economies is paramount.

The rest of this chapter highlights what needs to shift to implement an economy of well-being that restores and aligns us with our multidimensional selves and Mother Earth.

There are three critical pathways to attaining more sustainable measures of wealth: happiness, safety and presence. Happiness is an intrinsic quality we derive from loving and being loved. Safety is knowing we are grounded, secure and able to move forward because we are well-informed, discerning and action-oriented. Presence is the quality of being we bring to any situation where we respond and participate rather than disengage or avoid situations altogether. As the digital age grows, the likelihood of authentic connections might be threatened if these three precepts are not firmly internalised. As such, the three pathways can be helpful to get started (refer to Figure 8).

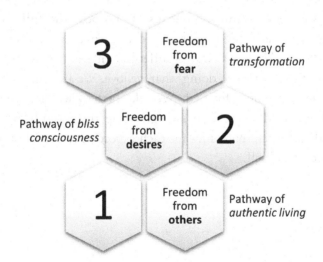

Figure 8: Access the actual source for joyful living aligned with purpose based on principles of unity, balance and harmony

In the first pathway, freedom from others, we look at the art of authentic living. In an economy of well-being, individuals invest their time and efforts in the opportunities best aligned with their natural talents and calling. When we each tap into our innate capabilities, we create unique offerings that can complement or serve new innovative functions from which a society can thrive. With information flows established on exact needs and requirements, inventors, creators and designers can be supported in their pursuits alongside regulators and enforcers, re-establishing balance in different ecosystems. Ensuring teams and leaders are plugged into their skill sets for industries facing disruptions can encourage healthy pivots within the organisation that help withstand emerging risks or trends. Overall, people regularly contribute to the economy with innovative offerings and creative endeavours that create more beneficial value for society.

Here, the stress is removed from needing to satisfy the expectations of others or society at large. Individuals are supported in developing their life purpose, which is encouraged rather than judged. Every exchange of talent is met with a need and purpose fulfilled. Such freedom cannot be understated. It might be the very defining nature of Industry 5.0 as we evoke humane features into our technology to build purpose-fit solutions. Capitalism is not the aim here but instead purpose and fulfilment. For this pathway to be realised, we must acknowledge that *wealth* must be understood as *multi-fold*. We do not suffer from ill health or a poor attitude towards contributing when doing what we love. We are more productive, and outcomes are more focused. We take better care of ourselves and ensure others are interested in strengthening their well-being as well. Figure 9 details these outcomes for each aspect when we align with our multi-dimensional self.

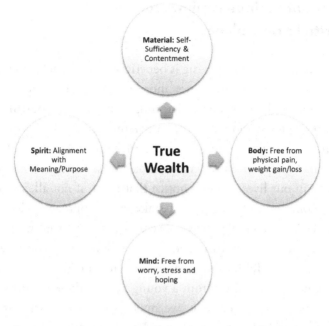

Figure 9: True wealth correlates to how we are living in this world with 'material', 'body', 'mind' and 'spirit' components equally considered

The 'material' component of wealth creation is perhaps the easiest to explain as it is our current means to an end. The more money we have, the more comforts/assets we can invest in and the more intergenerational wealth we can generate. What happens when we operate from a scarcity mindset? This is when we think something different cannot be done, people are too idealistic, and we have no room for error. Objectively speaking, we often see poor well-being from hoarding, fear-based protectionism and mistrust in others due to our identity as a 'wealthy individual'. Money blueprints that illuminate our spending habits also play a role. If we spend beyond our means, we will likely seek to earn/make more. Out of fear, many also hoard to remain 'wealthy'. We may also inherit specific ancestral scripts to support these mindsets based on 'we are separate' or 'we need to keep ourselves separate' to protect 'what's ours'. Therefore, the more we focus on other aspects of measuring wealth, the more clarity we can gain about our shadow selves. We can rewrite these stories.

An *abundance* mindset allows for co-*prosperity* to take place.

It recognises that while having is beneficial, giving back or supporting others to succeed is equally if not more meaningful. Such individuals are often seen in philanthropy or running nonprofits supporting critical social causes. The shadow aspects can manifest as a saviour complex, having unnecessary or unwanted guilt to help. Too much of a good thing also has the potential to create imbalances. As such, when we seek equilibrium in our lives, we will notice that most, if not all, social issues are highly complex and need a multistakeholder approach. Money alone cannot move the needle, especially if we have problems finding the needle in the haystack. Take education for girls in developing countries – the challenges are multi-fold, from access to the proper education, healthcare, and economic opportunities from a young age. In these countries, when ensuring education is accessible, we must also ensure their safety and health. This correlates with their 'freedom from others' potential. The more dependent or socially conservative we are on the support of others to succeed, the less likely we are to build wealth for ourselves and others. This is why social enterprises have targeted upskilling women across households with digital banking tools to ensure their incomes are saved and accessible by themselves rather than left in the hands of their 'caregivers' even if they are married.

The first step to developing equilibrium in the first pathway would be in our mind—*how do I/we think about ourselves regarding our relationships with people? Are we limited in any way, or what feedback have we received about our abilities that need rewriting?*

How does this make me feel in my body? Do I feel a sensation somewhere?

We are wealthy when we are worry-free, mature and clear-minded in the present moment. This requires a certain level of cleansing as we are also affected by collective thought forms from social media, our social circles and expectations to perform. When we step aside from always performing, especially to the likes and approval of others, we will feel a void. Suddenly, there is no external validation, which we have grown used to. We might start feeling 'alone' until we start attracting like-minded individuals. Like with other lifestyle changes, our thoughts will change the frequency and, in turn, how we feel. To feel authentically good, which is different from what we may tell ourselves when we are numb or in denial, actual wealth creation is in our minds. A healthy, balanced, and clear mind is more prosperous for self and others. There is an excellent strength in pursuing the unity of body-mind-spirit connection that many leave to retirement age, thinking there is no time or space for such authentic living. Pursuing a deeper spiritual connection between ourselves and nature is extremely important now. The more we elevate our consciousness, the more support we can feel daily. This self-awareness is better than our ego. In return, we are more aware of how to support Nature with conscious daily habits such as giving more than we take from her.

We start to operate from a detached state where we quit our compulsion to project onto others. We seek clarity in every situation and appreciate the many diverse perspectives we receive from around us. When we alchemise our field of activity, one field of body, one field of consciousness, we alchemise an ideal state of mind. One connected to the wisdom directly from the Source or the Godhead within us. During this time of elevated knowing, we need to detach from dogma. Even if we have rejected certain schools of thought growing up, we can still internalise unhealthy beliefs in the back of our minds. Any fear of patterning around feeling unsafe or overwhelmed is related to the mental, emotional and/or physical pain from our ancestors, compounded by our genetic dispositions and lifetimes of consequences from unaware actions taken. And this often has to manifest for us to acknowledge and heal; otherwise, it perpetuates as a never-ending cycle. We must do the work if we wish to be inside-out healed. We may find a strong and effective healer to work for us. Still, they cannot help us update our inner worlds as part of the crucial integration process, which unfolds after each healing – only we will know the nuances of the pain and lessons associated with us to embody its healing balm. And with practice, this will become more intuitive. We must remain persistent in its pursuit, even if it is initially painful.

Once we achieve equilibrium on all four fronts— material, body, mind, and spirit—we create true wealth for ourselves and others.

We show up as our best selves, harmoniously co-create with others, and effortlessly receive what life offers. We can respond with gratitude and generosity. Instead of needing to perform via imitation all the time, we live our self-expression freely and contribute to originality. We meet where we are until we find the cause of our disease, address it, thank it and let it go. This leads us to the second pathway of achieving freedom from desires. Once we achieve this foundational well-being state via the first pathway, we can explore the second pathway of bliss consciousness. In this realm, we realise that 'desires', in the form of our wants, hopes and dreams, stem from a place of lack. Most people on Earth constantly desire more, and this constant striving for something or someone drains our life force's energy. This is because we are distracted and largely dependent on whether we have something/someone, which can make us feel complete or empty in exchange. The spiritual truth is we are all complete and have the potential to achieve freedom from desires that keep us stuck in lower frequency thought forms such as 'unfairness', 'self-pity' and 'victimisation'. Here, ancestral imprints on our DNA play their part as much as collective thought forms that we plug into unconsciously when we are out and about.

When we realise the importance of simple happiness, feeling safe, and being 100 per cent present with ourselves or another, we understand the beauty of 'bliss consciousness'.

In this pathway, whatever will be will be, and we feel held in the moment. This would not be possible without the material safety and presence of thought we create for ourselves via the first pathway, which leads us to access simple happiness and well-being with freedom from desires. True wealth in this realm is non-materialistic, and we undertake more inner work journeys to explore our creative potential and how we can co-create better with others. The by-product of such a focus is an inspiring and uplifting ecstasy for collective well-being. This is when we can access the third pathway of transformation—freedom from fear— when we can look fear directly in the eye and see it as what it is—an energy charge. Fear does not hold us back when we rewrite the script, change the thought pattern, or go through a new experience. When our overall energy transforms, it invigorates, and we feel…free.

We actively seek answers to questions like: *Where do I not feel free?*

Where do I play the victim?

What are my agendas?

We transform old patterns of self-harm, self-neglect, and self-betrayal into elevated states of being: self-love, self-awareness, and self-esteem. We take responsibility for our actions and know we control our thoughts, spoken words, and actions. We are in control of our emotions and feelings in our bodies. We trust ourselves more each day as we remember there is no danger in the unknown. With this growing self-awareness, we innately inspire others to empower themselves.

Fear has many benefits, such as restricting and limiting our options, which are meant to make us feel safe. It gives us the impetus to survive when

**we are in danger. It is that trigger to our sixth sense
that says, 'Something is not right here; get out.'**

Fear stems from survival mentality because, historically, having options
was not possible or accessible. For many of us, ancestral stories and cultural
attitudes keep us locked for fear of something going wrong. These are
significant, unknown hurdles for us to cross before we even realise this is
something we want to do for ourselves. This is where we must be brave in
seeing things as they are without judging. Many situations or people are
the way they are primarily due to a lack of awareness. When we raise our
consciousness, we help others see their potential reflected in them. That is
when a collective change can start to take place.

Deepak Chopra's book *Abundance: The Inner Path to Wealth* illuminates
the conditions needed for our *dharma* or the right way for living to unfold.
It will require 1) clear intention, 2) no confusion, 3) the highest evolutionary
path available to us for growth, 4) no harm done to others, and 5) the best
outcome for everyone involved.[21] Similar to the Japanese concept of *Ikigai*,
we can ascertain our *dharma* based on what we are good at, what we love
to do, how it best fits with what the world needs, and whether we can get
paid for it. We must start, for this is the source of true inner affluence, as
our *dharma* will guide us from within. 'Money' or status, as a concept,
drops its significance when we feel fully empowered to overcome any
situation with the support of creative intelligence. Being in line with this
flow opens us up to infinite possibilities. We must balance our analytical
left brains with our intuitive right brains for creative intelligence to flow
more effortlessly. This would require us to develop our feminine qualities
of receptivity, active listening and inner silence via our right brain as our
yin aspect flows through the *yang's* outward execution momentum to
achieve our true satisfaction.

Self-reliance stems from raising our inner awareness. We will benefit
from finding the middle ground in every situation by ensuring we are not
living on either end of the Light/Dark spectrum. This equilibrium state
will ensure we are grounded in the practical realities of our times and doing
our best with what we have. A state of mutual understanding and support

---

[21]   Chopra, D., 'Abundance: The Inner Path to Wealth', Harmony, March 1 2022
       [audiobook].

suspends judgment and blame. It avoids labelling situations or people and aims at creative solutions instead. Such a state is dignity-conscious, focusing on levelling the playing field by building equitable structures. This is the foreseeable future once we start evolving and spiritually awakening. Table 4 shows the differences in perception needed to adopt a holistic wealth understanding to a fulfilling life.

< Finding The Equilibrium State
in being *compassionate, transparent and connected* >

Material	Body	Mind	Spirit
True wealth:	*True wealth:*	*True wealth:*	*True wealth:*
o New experiences	o Vitality	o Present	o Endless creativity
o New growth	o Longevity	o Zero-point state	o Unconditional love
opportunities	o Perfect Health	between worry and	o Bliss Consciousness
o Self-sufficiency	o Movement	hope	o Gratitude
o Self-mastery		o Lucidity	
Light aspects:	*Light aspects:*	*Light aspects:*	*Light aspects:*
o Generous	o Surrendered	o Growth-oriented	o Fearless
o Detached	o Open	o Present	o Loving
Shadow aspects:	*Shadow aspects:*	*Shadow aspects:*	*Shadow aspects:*
o Calculative	o Controlling	o Fixed mindset	o Fearful
o Attached	o Closed	o Shallow	o Withholding

*Table 4: Redefining what true wealth could
mean for us at an individual level*

Duality consciousness is thinking one state is better, often ignoring or shunning our shadow or darker aspects into oblivion. The spiritual truth is we are all made of positive and negative aspects, and many of us are here to clear these stories that have been part of the collective journey for many generations. The sooner we realise our duties to ourselves, our families and our communities, the sooner we can all start living more conscious and harmonious lives. The worst is when we allow various forms of 'corruption' and 'fear' that permeate our society to limit us in realising true wealth.

This is when the following questions may be helpful:

Do we give or hoard?

Do we embrace or reject?

Do we feel enough or need more constantly?

When we ignore this opportunity to heal our inner world, we say yes to living life with the *status quo*: numbing, armouring, distraction, and blame, to name a few. We need to meet ourselves where we are by looking into how we cope and doing the inner work to *make us feel whole and safe again* because no one else can do this for us.

To redefine wealth in this regard, we each need to trace our roots back to the beginning to plant seeds and grow roots that can sustain for some time. Many of us living in urban cities, away from our ancestral lands or unaware of where we originate from, face a more profound crisis of disconnect within ourselves, and these times will call for us to reconcile this issue.

Connecting with Our Lineage

We all come from somewhere, and we need to acknowledge our past and origin stories no matter how challenging, painful, or vague they might be. Self-realisation is incomplete until we reconcile with all fragments of ourselves, including our ancestral and soul lineages.

A) Ancestral

We each come from specific family lines, and it will be helpful to draw out a family tree if you have all the information. Otherwise, listing our immediate family unit, including those estranged or departed from us, would be helpful.

o Set up a ceremonial space to centre ourselves in a calm, healing environment

o Light a candle or place pictures of family members in front of you, if available

o Make a prayer to share your loving intention to connect with your loved ones

o Announce your name and relation to the loved ones, significantly for grandparents who departed, for instance (while this is not necessary as our Higher Soul is always in sync with Spirit and the souls of our loved ones, it can help us to stay grounded and intentional in our spiritual practices)

o Share with them your experiences and how you would like their help to heal the dynamic by honouring their pain/sacrifice/efforts

o Breathe in, breathe out and relax to tune into your intuition

o Hear them speak to you by writing the first thoughts or images that come to your mind in your journal

o Remember their guidance will always be loving and gentle. Any unhelpful or disconcerting feedback could mean there is an interference

o Do not be afraid and invoke your guardian angel or higher power you pray to clear the space and restore harmony for you

- o   Recentre yourself by drinking a glass of water
- o   When comfortable, try again by shifting position or after some time

B)   Soul

- o   As eternal facets of the One Source, we exist through time and space
- o   It is commonplace for our souls to have lived different lifetimes on Earth and other star systems
- o   Sit in a ceremonial space to connect with yourself
- o   Tune into your breath and have a journal prepared
- o   Ask your Higher Self or Guides to share information that you need to know about your past lives
- o   Close your eyes and allow any visuals or information to come to you in your mind's eye
- o   Write down what you see without thinking or rationalising
- o   In the beginning, it could be keywords or random images – this is ok
- o   Once you are done, thank your Higher Self and Guides
- o   For those who are more comfortable invoking your Akashic Records, perform the pathway prayer and open to receive guidance
- o   Please note that while information may seem unclear and even confusing initially, the signs and symbols will eventually make sense in time; we have to be patient and trust ourselves
- o   Again, if there are any disturbances or interferences with your meditation, please ensure to clear your auric field or space with sage or *palo santo* before meditating again
- o   Do not be afraid. Always invoke a Higher Power through a mantra or invocation to oversee all of your sessions to feel safe

Happiness stems from knowing we can rely on creative intelligence at any time to help us navigate life and find meaningful opportunities for evolutionary growth and self-mastery. This is happiness that stems from growing. Growing is not always linear; it is sometimes painful but rewarding whenever we look back. Harnessing safety when we embark on any change initiative is therefore essential. This is telling ourselves that we are enough, even if we do not believe it at first, and that we can take care of ourselves. If we make mistakes, we forgive ourselves. We remind ourselves never to harm or abandon ourselves because this is crucial for our inner child and overall emotional well-being. If a change initiative is too challenging, we can slow down, we can pause.

The frequency of feeling safe attracts loving or unloving experiences towards us.

When we realise this fundamental truth, we can transform it for our betterment and that of others. When we are safe, we will not demand others take care of us, and we will heal co-dependency wounds. We will know how to show up with presence because we understand the only moment that matters is now, and we have to make the most of it by allowing it to happen and flow through us as we transform it in return. When widening our consciousness, we encounter old stories and limiting beliefs from internalised dogma or social conditioning. By bringing our attention to the present moment and the feeling or pain our body is experiencing, we can unlock extra-sensory insight for our liberation. This requires clear intention and following through with our deepest desire to love ourselves wholeheartedly like never before and to be one with all that is.

Back to Basics Body, Heart and Mind Scan

1. Feeling something? Sit in a meditative pose and tune in to your breath for beginners and experienced meditators – the mind's eye
2. Feel the feeling. Get curious about it - what happened to make you feel this way? Has it happened before? Is it a recurring pattern?
3. Notice where else pain might manifest in your body (perhaps a backache, etc.)—get curious about that.

4. List everything down along with the date so that we can track these symptoms and incidences.

5. If these emotions and mental states recur, please note that they are more likely to be ancestral or karmic patterns. We all inherit the collective shadows of previous generations. These manifest in our DNA, as Richard Rudd, Creator of the Gene Keys, elaborates in his 'Seven Sacred Seals Course'.

6. Suspending all judgment is necessary as our ancestors did not know better or were victims of their circumstances. Move into a state of compassion and think of the opposite emotion or state of being to nullify and heal this old wound. The belief that all matter has yin and yang qualities will help integrate this kind of shadow work better.

7. [Bonus] Connect with your inner child to see how they feel about the situation – you will know this feeling in your heart or belly. Some may have a vision of your younger self in your mind's eye. Say hi, connect, ask them what they need, and complete their request. Most times, because of this locked-up pain, our child aspect had to grow up sooner than we would have liked or could not express our childlike enthusiasm for life as enthusiastically as we would have liked – hold space for whatever desires come through to rebuild our relationship with ourselves.

Refocusing our attention requires a present-moment focus where we are fully immersed in our lives. We are responding to everything coming at us or making conscious choices about what we wish to do and going about them. Whatever comes up – good or bad is seen as a reflection from within us, and we meet it with curiosity to heal it. We also choose to make choices that uplift us and others around us in every moment. This may not lead us to instant joy or bliss mode, but as we sharpen this intention, the breakthroughs get more manageable, we heal faster, and the road ahead seems smoother. It will require us to surrender to our desires and know that the universe knows better than we do to deliver beyond what we can imagine possible. Like water that does not cling yet shapes the rocks and terrains it traverses, so are we meant to flow. Every moment, every day, we can ask ourselves two central questions:

1)   How nourished am I feeling right now?

2)   How lost/disconnected/lonely am I feeling right now?

We cannot change our behaviours without being in sync with ourselves. Blockages in our physical body can manifest as physical discomfort, which, left unaddressed, can cause further pain to accumulate.[22] This is why raising awareness to notice our bodies, hearts, and minds can go a long way as a preventive health measure. We do even better when we can align ourselves with Earth's seasons and the cycles of our solar and lunar systems. We will be able to work together with Nature to know when to take rest when to move, when to build and when to let it all go. Acknowledging our humanity and, honestly, our physical vulnerability ensures our inherent circadian rhythms flow more optimally. As cyclical beings, we ride different waves of emotions as the seasons change; let us soften, metaphorically wilt away by grieving all that has served us, making room for new seeds to grow and harvest, only to repeat the cycle. Let us welcome *regenerative* approaches to *sustaining ourselves and others.*

---

[22]   *Please note that while this book does not discuss the chakra and meridian systems in depth, plenty of literature online supports your query search, if any. It is important to note where each chakra corresponds to which area of our bodies will tremendously help the healing process. When we know where the root cause for physical pain is coming from, we can better diagnose and make lifestyle changes or select the healing modalities to help us resolve the pain, once and for all.*

Self **Deprivation**
*A 'negative'
extreme where
we keep
ourselves in lack
mode in order to
future-proof
ourselves from
any crisis*

 Self **Indulgence**
*A 'positive'
extreme where
we are in living in
the now with a
disconnect from
thinking about
consequences*

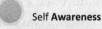 Self **Awareness**
*A balanced state
where we are
living in the
infinite now with
an awareness to
pick the most
uplifting
possibility for our
path forward*

We understand co-prosperity when we can slow down enough to sync with the seasons and the cycles of our bodies as we age, recover and rebuild, especially after any trauma. It is not at the expense of ourselves or others but an inward journey of outward exuberance. Through this reckoning with our inner depths, we learn the importance of patience and wisdom, which will eventually come through. We are here on Earth to do this so that we can walk around as clear mirrors for others to do their work. Any darker emotions such as shame, unworthiness, disappointment, insecurity or plain lethargy are there for us to work through firstly physically. Please venture outdoors and do some physical movement or activity to shake this energy up. It is like the residue of hot cocoa that has settled to the bottom, which needs to be stirred to clarify why it is present to emerge. Once we are mentally ready, ask ourselves what about this situation is scary for me? Figure 10 offers the steps we might take to deal with healing.

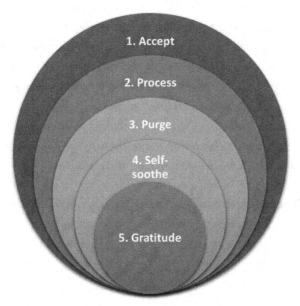

Figure 10: A healing crisis often requires us to undergo layers of shedding to uncover deep gratitude for the re-discovery of our true self through union with our Higher Self[23]

Five steps to get through a healing crisis: *A healing crisis can happen when we overload our physical body's nervous system by over-attempting purification work with insufficient integration. It can also occur if we do not begin our work on what is surfacing for us. Our bodies usually undergo a health crisis, so we must realise, reprioritise, and focus on holistic health.*

1. **Accept** space for ourselves - Are we aware and available to grieve* our every ending/beginning in life?

   _____

   _____

---

[23]   *Higher self also known as oversoul, holy spirit, creative intelligence, etc.*

Grief: there is a natural tendency to relegate this emotion to when a loved one or someone passes. However, the reality is grief does not need death to occur to show up. It shows in the powerful realisations of how our dignity has been denied. It shows how we must let go of what no longer serves us. In this regard, thanking what has left us with all of our hearts can be a helpful ritual to reframe the 'pain' as something positive and fulfilling in our lives. As cyclical beings, the ebbs and flows of life will help us be more accustomed to these realities soon enough if we allow it.

2. **Process** old trauma language* / fears – What do we catch ourselves commonly saying when we are hurt that sounds like something we heard growing up, which we internalised?

   _____

   _____

Trauma language refers to phrases and words that trigger us or that we project onto others when deeply saddened by someone's action. This often comes across as rage or anger when it is simply language we have internalised from the environments we have grown up in. Recognising what our trauma language is is our first step to uncovering what we might have repressed in our psyche about what may have happened sometime back during childhood. Language can show us our way back to ourselves if we listen and help each other realise what we sometimes say in moments of disappointment and anguish (mostly with ourselves).

3. **Purge*** through processing—How can we let go of what is holding us back? Do daily reflection, sharing with a trusted friend, and therapy help?

   _____

   _____

Purge: a cathartic process that allows us to witness certain truths in a way only we can acknowledge through another, be it on film, story writing or reenactment of our own lives. We get to be the protagonist in the show, allowing ourselves to feel the difficult emotions pent up within us. In this moment of release, we liberate ourselves from shame. We permit ourselves to

*be synchronous with global healing occurring around us. Allowing ourselves
to relive these painful occurrences in a medium of choice (i.e. movie, TV
Show, novel) helps us let go.*

4. **Self-soothe*** to heal – How can I be a parent to myself and
   meet my hurt self where it is needed?

   _____

   _____

**Self-soothe: our mature adult self must compassionately meet our younger
self to hold space and accept what has occurred to transmute the pain
into new realisations. In this case, the transmutation to something more
uplifting, heroic, and survival-focused shows us that we can overcome and
move on. But first, it requires us to meet ourselves at a level where we
understand what is happening so that we can take the next appropriate
steps to resolve and return to one consciousness or love.*

5. Practice **gratitude** for purification* and awareness building. What
   am I thankful for in this challenging lesson? How has it helped me
   grow to become a more loving person? If I am not there yet, how
   may I hold space for myself to sit with these difficult emotions and
   forgive myself and others so that I can move on?

   _____

   _____

**Purification: historically, purity has not had a good reputation for the
means and methods used to enforce it and encourage it out of us. This
time, we get to choose how and what needs to be purified by first accepting
all parts of ourselves and promising not to abandon ourselves again. It
begins with the acknowledgement of both our light and dark aspects to
start the actual work of integrating the two and alchemising them to a
more apparent state of being where we are aware of our faults and those
of others and encourage each other to start loving ourselves by raising the
vibrational quality of what serves our life. By aligning with Light, we open
the gateways for fresh perspectives and optimistic, positive visions for our
lives that we deserve, whether we first believe it or not.*

We deserve to keep moving forward in the most responsible way possible for ourselves and others involved.

There is only one predominant base feeling: fear that sets us back from anything. Understanding and allowing ourselves to be scared is necessary, and then meeting ourselves to work through solutions will be the next step. There is no problem without a solution, except the solutions will vary depending on how expanded our consciousness is. And it is ok if we change our minds as we move along to update our trajectories. We are aligning with the highest timelines and vibration possible for us. When we heal, we open up to more love. Let us persist.

PART II

WE MAKE THE SYSTEMS

IV

REIMAGINE SAFETY

The World Economic Forum's Global Risks Report 2024 made a notable shift towards examining the impacts of technological advances and economic volatility.[24] While the core issues of energy, food supply, human rights, and climate goals have persisted over the past few years, 2024 shows a more complex relationship between technological and economic interdependencies, requiring a more nuanced understanding of global risks.[25] Fragile economies and strained international cooperation make us increasingly *susceptible* to disruptions. Even minor shocks could push our systems beyond their resilience limits. As such, given today's complex risks, safety needs to be reimagined, particularly at an individual level.

In the second half of this book, we examine how we can build our systems to make the necessary accommodations for all to prosper in the coming decades. This will require tremendous willpower as we rebalance ourselves to a state of inner strength and resolve to follow through on our self-transformation, self-development, and autonomy.

---

24 World Economic Forum, 'Global Risks Report 2024', 10 January 2024, https:// www.weforum.org/publications/global-risks-report-2024/ (Accessed 14 June 2024).

25 World Economic Forum, 'Global Risks Report 2024'.

This requires us to think about harmonic resonance at a deeper level –

how may we tune in to the 'right' *resonance* and ensure we receive what we need to write new stories here on Earth?

Resonance builds when we think, feel and are one with what we wish to manifest. It is thinking in the form of questions, feeling in the form of closure and being in the form of wellness. Resonance requires this trinity to be in place for it to come through. When our minds are occupied, we are unlikely to resonate with messages coming through for us. Instead, our interest might be piqued if what we feel is addressed in some way or another.

In this trinity, feelings have precedence. When we think of closure, we can achieve it by addressing a feeling and embodying the state of mind and heart we wish to achieve. The thing about awakening is that we take time to build resonance with the material or wisdom around us, be it on YouTube, blogs, or websites. We may go for quick fixes, especially if someone offers light language, energy, sound healing services, and more. We are self-healing, and the more we attune to these modalities, the more internal resonance we build to understand and connect inwardly ourselves. As we make these inner channels for deeper resonance to occur within us at all times, we will naturally connect when we awaken our multidimensionality, the temporal and existential space.

Our *vibration* attracts our *current* point of attraction.

Harmonic resonance, in line with our dharma and co-prosperity, invites new perspectives into our existence. With this widening of perspectives, we consciously manifest heaven on Earth. This is the 5-dimensional vibrational reality that is available to us. It will require us to keep returning to ourselves and nature. The more we commit to our lives here on Earth, the more grounded we feel. We will not be swayed by popular opinion, regardless of how reputable the source is. We learn only to trust ourselves. But this does not mean we walk around with noise-cancelling headphones, either. Our external worlds need our attention as much as we ground from within. Ensuring we are available for others to seek support in co-creating solutions is essential. We are not meant to feel isolated or live apart from what we need to connect our inner dots. In union, and primarily through our relationships, we will accelerate our growth on how to grow together.

We are all here to seek wisdom, especially from Gaia and nature beings, and heal ourselves to realise our destiny. We cannot do this without understanding our inner world, and what has caused it to be in the state, it is in right now. If one is unsure of what your inner world looks like, look around you and the events occurring in your life with an objective eye, non-judgement and keen compassion: you will notice the fissures, the recurring pain cycles and the constant dramas we put ourselves through to be seen and heard, feel nourished or protected by someone else. We forget we have those reserves within us to furnish our lighthouse to be as sustainably lit as possible, should we dare to tend to our inner gardens. Figure 11 shows us what we need to heal, how to reparent and be there for ourselves.

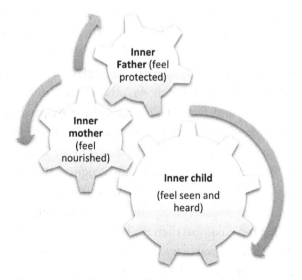

Figure 11: Safety stems from our core healing nexus consisting of our inner child and parents

When we embark on our healing journeys, a lot has to be purged, and inevitably, we will be attracting recurring events to see how we deal with them as we clear out our emotional and mental blockages around the people or situations that trigger us. As we progress, these events will irritate or annoy us less, and we will have more control over how we respond and begin to see where the other person is coming from to heal the relationship dynamics. We will reach a whole new level of understanding and peace that surpasses this understanding simultaneously. However, we must be gentle with ourselves if our vision of life is still far from what we live. Great things take time, and healing deserves our attention. We may be able to accelerate it during special cosmic events such as eclipses and portals; however, our Higher Self knows how to regulate our actions toward healing so that we are not in a healing crisis from attempting to leap more than we can handle. There are moments for every epiphany, and we have the patience for it.[26]

Our inner mother and father represent the roots of our divine feminine and masculine energy, respectively. This means our behaviours in our gendered roles/sexuality tend to derive from our relationship with our caregivers (often parents or grandparents) and how they modelled the gendered role expectations to us. This is not to say we do not develop our consciousness regarding how to be from an early age - we do, and that is often where the initial conflicts begin within us. Are we this or that? As adults, we now have the power to be authentic and to seek a middle ground regardless of how we were treated or shown otherwise in our formative years. Our divine masculine and feminine energy further shapes how we show up. When slightly skewed towards one end, we tend to attract life lessons or experiences that help us realise what is missing to reach a more balanced state of being. The challenge would be to recognise the significance of these experiences and learn what we must learn from them to avoid them from repeating. It took me several repetitive events to realise the recurring patterns, each time more painful than the last because I was semi-aware but was not sure how or why I was attracting these similar types of experiences.

Further, the importance of the divine masculine in creating safety and containment for the receptive flow of our intuition through our divine feminine cannot be understated. We often use our divine masculinity

---

[26]   *Please note this book does not call for any drastic action to be taken but to simply tune into ourselves more to get the answers we often seek externally or in others, which can be confusing or misleading if our discernment skills are challenged for a variety of reasons.*

to force our way through life, do as much as possible and achieve what we think is necessary. This curtails our divine feminine from showing up because all that matters is we are doing something, not knowing that by softening our disposition, we can allow our divine feminine to help us find a more aligned way of living, which often involves less rushing and more intuitive flow with what is needed around us. Table 5 shows how we can reparent ourselves and return to wholeness regarding our divine Self. While typecasting the divine masculine as the Inner Father is more straightforward, for instance, it will be inaccurate. The divine masculine is in all of us regardless of our gender. Nevertheless, for the sake of simplicity, we refer to a parental unit as our fundamental understanding of a heterosexual family unit to serve as an example of how we need not look for external comfort or validation when we have it within us to survive and overcome in meeting ourselves where we are at.

	Inner child	Inner Father	Inner Mother
Intention	To hear and see me	To protect me	To nourish me
What We Can Do	**Visualise** your inner child and sense what they need by meditating with them.	**Discern** better by doing our due diligence to ensure our emotional safety will not be compromised	**Prioritise** our well-being (eat well, eat on time, hydrate frequently, rest well and hug ourselves)
	Identify and heal childhood trauma/pain narratives.	**Hold space** for our challenging times, awkward emotions and deep pain; we will get through it.	**Trust** that we are not alone, know when something is wrong, and can walk away.
	Overcome fears of abandonment, neglect, etc with self-care	**Do** make consistent efforts to take good care of ourselves by investing in unlearning what we may have inherited	**Integrate** what we are constantly learning about ourselves to embrace a new, more wholesome version of us daily.

Table 5: Our initial precepts of safety begin in childhood, and we can reparent ourselves to heal and be there for ourselves like never before

When we exercise this inner identification of the power of creative energy within us to heal ourselves, we can visualise ourselves safe, taken care of and recognised by ourselves. This comes at no additional cost or risk. We must put aside time to clear all the inroads to our heart space.

Recognising how the divine masculine and feminine energy plays up in our behaviours and beliefs can be highly instrumental in our growth journeys. The tendency to be 'imbalanced' stems from unresolved trauma. As we heal, this unlocks pathways to our balanced states, which further propels us forward into what we have been called to do in this lifetime. Through healing my traumas and wounds, the self-discovery of rebalancing what is important to me came through as I worked on my wounded divine feminine energy and overemphasised divine masculine energy. I was overgiving and underappreciative of myself: an undesirable state of wellness involving lots of giving without much receptiveness. I worked consciously to align my thoughts, beliefs and actions with a balanced outlook of what is happening around me instead of taking on others' burdens as mine.

Further, the nature of our divine feminine and masculine energies can help us explain where we are stuck, co-dependent, or interdependent in our relationships. The latter - interdependence is achieved when we recognise a balance within ourselves and seek out others with complementary strengths to work towards progress together. We will not have all the abilities because we are meant to show up in unique ways, which is why we are meant to partner and grow with others. Knowing what we are good at and where we contribute best as early in life as possible helps us pursue more aligned goals for ourselves. We can show up for ourselves and others feeling more fulfilled. Feeling stuck or co-dependent are imbalanced states. We tend to be stuck if we believe what we think is the best and only way forward. We tend to lose the support of others along the way and might close up, causing us to stay stuck. Co-dependent, on the other hand, is when we give our power to someone because we either believe they have some control over us or that we are not enough. These states, while 'normal' given we do not live in a perfect set-up, are detrimental to our spiritual growth as they mean we will feel a sense of lack manifesting somewhere. To heal this, we must reclaim our power from others. For most of us, this is a bewildering thing to do in the first place, as we might be too entangled in a situation to know where our boundaries start and end with another.

As such, highly sensitive individuals and empaths (such as myself) must understand the importance of self-love when protecting our energy exchanges with others. If we often feel drained and exhausted, this is a sign of leakage, and we will need to look at our boundaries. This also requires a more in-depth understanding of our environments, how we are showing up, and what is necessary for us to show up. If we are performing and not being authentic, it often takes a more significant toll on us. If we have to fit in somehow, this will also take an additional toll. Table 6 shows how we may return to our balanced states by being aware of and healing the behaviours that no longer serve us.

Imbalanced Masculine	Balanced Masculine	Imbalanced Feminine	Balanced Feminine
Dominant	Facilitative	Submissive	Secure
Unyielding	Open-minded	Closed	Open-hearted
Suspicious	Cautious	Easy-going	Focused
Overbearing	Understanding	Sacrificial	Boundaries
Lost	Structured	Stuck	Progressive
Forceful	Allowing	Manipulative	Transparent
Angry	Centred	Vengeful	Forgiving
Indecisive	Committed	Controlling	Surrendered
Withholding	Trusting	Rejecting	Receptive
Ambitious	Contented	Scattered	Attuned
Distant	Present	Entangled	Detached
Opinionated	Clarifying	Assuming	Curious

Table 6: Seeking balance between our divine masculine and feminine aspects is key if we wish to let go of 'limiting narratives' that no longer serve us

We are all working on our spiritual ascension towards greater understanding, compassion, and kindness for all, as well as deeper harmonic resonance within ourselves and the collective. The main aim of this process is for us to achieve a higher vibrational state of being and receive frequency downloads from our higher self and other Light entities working with humanity to help us ascend towards unconditional love. This higher vibration state is an unshakable belief in oneself to integrate anything in life, especially our darker aspects of individual and collective shadows. The end state we are all striving for is perfect balance and harmony in terms of what makes us feel safe first. This is regarding our emotional, mental, physical, spiritual, inter-relational and community aspects. Secondly, we can only achieve perfect balance and harmony when we let go of expectations. This is the union state where we are detached from the outcomes of our efforts and are worry-free, trusting that in the present moment, we will know how to proceed next. Unconditional love naturally ensues as a by-product because we free ourselves from judgement and purify our hearts as we learn to let go of what no longer serves us, including our safety blankets from yesteryears. This leads us into the sanctum of trust within us to unlock our true, unshakeable state of being, which leads to a secure sense of stability that allows us to be prudent, clear in thought, and assured of support and love.

Figure 12 below shows a systematic breakdown of what happens as we ascend, and perhaps you may identify with a particular phase you are in right now. The "Roadblock / Test / Challenge Energy" is the most crucial of these phases. Most of us are experiencing this now as we are regularly bombarded with news stories of worldwide injustices and sensationalised happenings that make us wonder what the world is turning to. This is distracting as we know it, yet many of us are addicted to knowing, thinking it will keep us safe, when, on the contrary, it is detracting us from our spiritual growth towards higher levels of knowing from within.

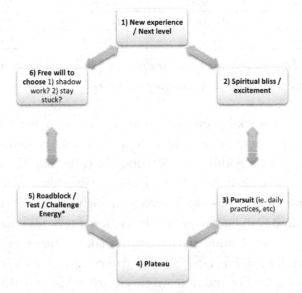

Figure 12: The typical mindset/behavioural tendency that emerges when we focus on our spiritual evolution/growth process

When we do not feel safe, we are anxious, creating dis-ease energy. Instead of helping ourselves focus on safety, we might fight by catastrophising, flight by abandoning ourselves or freeze with inertia to move forward. What this creates firstly is tension in our mental and emotional bodies. We are constricting because we are feeling unsafe, further perpetuated by our minds. Instead, letting go and surrendering is something we need to get used to.

Let's stop to reflect:

- At which stage of this cycle am I currently? And why?

  _____

  _____

- If we are unaware of which phase we are at,

  o Have I been through any recent spiritual experiences in nature, at work or in a deep conversation with a trusted friend?

    _____

    _____

  o Have I sensed a feeling of resonance or self-reckoning?

    _____

    _____

  o Where do I seek out safe spiritual experiences?

    _____

    _____

  o What makes me feel better?

    _____

    _____

"Safety and all notions of it came to the fore many times through my life experiences – what it means to an average person, how we take it for granted when we have it, and what we do when we do not have it."[27]

Using AI for shadow work:

- Please remember before initiating any conversation with an AI chatbot that it is not a real person
- Please type in clear statements (see example below) to receive a relevant response
- Example: "Today, I experienced (a specific event or interaction) and felt (the emotions that arose from that experience), which left me questioning (the thoughts or beliefs that came up). I would like to know how to heal."

Additional prompts:

- **Trigger Identification**: What specific part of the experience triggered the emotional response? Was there a particular word, action, or situation that stood out?
- **Beliefs and Patterns**: What underlying beliefs about ourselves or the world might be connected to this experience? Have we noticed any recurring patterns in similar situations?
- **Physical Sensations**: What physical sensations did we notice alongside the emotional response? Did we feel tense, relaxed, fatigued, etc.?
- **Reactions and Responses**: How did we react in the moment? Did we express our feelings, withdraw, or respond in another way?
- **Lessons and Insights**: What do we think this experience is trying to teach us? Is there a lesson or insight that stands out to us?

---

[27]   D. Kaur, 'The Action Gap: Business Strategies for Co-Prosperity', 2024, Partridge, p.114.

- **Support and Resources**: Who or what can support us in our healing journey? Are there books, practices, or people we can turn to for guidance?
- **Self-Compassion**: How can we show kindness and compassion regarding this experience? What comforting words would we say to a friend in a similar situation?

Modern living has its conveniences and disadvantages when it comes to healing. We can just as easily post on social media or rant about it to a friend as we can sit with ourselves to process with zero-point meditation. Every situation has its dualistic characteristics, and the more we train ourselves to see things as clearly as possible, the greater clarity we can receive on how we ought to think, feel, and be. Regarding addressing the "Roadblock / Test / Challenge Energy," Figure 13 offers steps a) to f) to guide us when we feel stuck when ascending to the next level. Please note the ascension journey is focused on helping us achieve our highest potential by clearing out what no longer serves us. Each new level brings a new understanding for us to discern, decide and act in more loving, aligned ways with our true selves. This is why we invest in this transformative work. As with most healing work, there is no right or wrong. We must trust our intuition even if it seems to guide us towards uncomfortable experiences. Our job is to understand the situation we are judging (perhaps even without realising), why we are uncomfortable (are our values being challenged?), and how we may transmute and feel better.

Is a reframe required, or does overcoming an unknown fear need to occur?

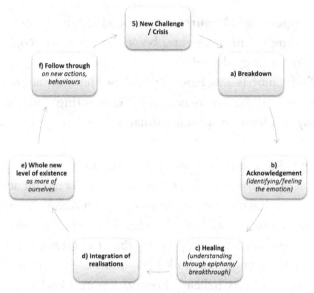

Figure 13: Following these steps can help effectively integrate and heal the challenging energy

When we choose to be brave and address this phase of the spiritual journey, we choose to heal, resolve an old story, and move on to a new beginning or cycle of growth. When we ignore, deny, or deflect this energy, we start to feel stuck with deeply embedded emotions flaring up for us to overcome. The good news is that the more precise we are, the more stoic we become about the process; it is less emotionally charged, and we can internalise the lessons we need to learn and integrate them into our daily lives without hesitation. It may still be lethargic energy, but only so that we may slow down to be still with this moment of reckoning before we go on with our busy lives again, where a new beginning awaits. Therefore, accumulatively, as we ascend across our lifetime, we will eventually be able to work on our immediate family and ancestral and collective wounds to help others succeed. This process unearths the many layers of safety that have been affected through the ages by historic wars, famine, poverty, exile/displacement/migration, social mobility, and more. Our ancestors' experiences are also in our DNA, and when we activate our dormant spiritual DNA, we can see which of our experiences are theirs and start to heal them with their help.

We all come with certain baggage, which mainly defines our life predispositions. We need to acknowledge their source when we are working on transmuting these unhelpful frequencies to more beneficial vibrations. We need to go back and come forth to this moment again. This can occur with a simple mindfulness practice of thanking and witnessing our family line go as far as we allow and return with heartfelt gratitude for all that has transpired between time and space. We may not know the details, but if we are privy to the history of our times, we have also gone through tough times and overcame them. Our family lines have persisted every millennium, and we have experienced tremendous hardships and lives taken away. This has left imprints in us where we feel this heightened need to protect what is ours by hoarding and protecting our families because there was once they were taken away from us (and might still be happening in current times). We might even threaten to harm another or remove them completely. And this takes a toll on our soul.

Our soul knows that we are one with all beings at the spiritual level. Somehow, as we go down to the physical level, the situation remains confused and fear-based. We are not predators; we are not victims either. We have simply been playing this reel in our minds, thinking that this is a reality and how we are expected to be. Anxiety could, therefore, come from unprocessed survivor's guilt, which leads to a need to constantly do something to make up for opportunities that were not available to our predecessors. Anxiety could also mean overcompensating our identities, especially if we come from ethnic minority backgrounds so that we can fit in or not be typecast into a specific stereotype. We want to fit in, we want to belong, and we want to feel accepted. Instead, we end up constantly proving our worth or justifying why we take up space, which can be disempowering if we internalise this behaviour as a habit.

We are sovereign beings born with our personal integrity fully intact until we started giving parts of our power away to 'fit in'. In some dominant cultures, power is taken away from us so that we can all homogenise and not disrupt 'the whole'. Working with our consciousness will address all these conflicting actions to unify the opposites and emerge whole again. Most of us are numb to new challenges or crises, which could mean we repeat similar cycles for ourselves, not knowing why this is so, or we create physical disease by not addressing the challenging energy emerging to the surface to be cleared.

History has also given rise to a peculiar phenomenon of females harbouring wounded divine masculine energies and males harbouring wounded divine feminine energies. For individuals who identify as non-binary, please pardon the arbitrary distinction of Self and map out your weaker tendencies as your wound to heal. Patriarchy has caused most males in our collectives to lose touch with their feminine aspects in the race to be alpha leaders of their pack. This has resulted in women giving their power away only to fight for it back, causing us to overemphasise our masculine energy to be heard, seen or be part of any decision-making table. We can and need to reclaim these lost aspects of ourselves now. Balance is required for Industry 5.0 and New World consciousness.

The fear of 'will we be harmed' also needs to be healed now. It impacts us at an individual, organisational, societal, and even global level. We are willing to invest billions into defence and insurance to withstand the shocks of unpredictable actors despite our linear growth-focused markets with their inflationary pressures. How can we evolve from this state of arrested tension within us that does not serve our nervous systems well to think we might be harmed at any time or if something unexpected will emerge for us to deal with it as swiftly as possible?

Our humanity is important, and we need to remember this essence now. This pure essence makes us who we are. All of us are vulnerable regardless of our socio-economic status or identity. At any point, markets can crash, new regulations emerge, and faster, leaner start-ups can upend our business. To stay agile and undeterred in the face of change lies in realising our personal and collective humanity in all that we do. A government that considers the nuances of its social protection policies ensures its citizens are assured to stay resilient. A business that invests in talent development and cross-functional collaboration ensures business continuity by propagating growth opportunities from within and creating new business potential for its stakeholders. This viability of how we can start to show up is limitless when we realise what is at stake: we are ALL in this together, including Nature and its associated ecosystems from which our products and services are derived.

The shadow aspects of our lives, business operations and governance are no longer to be feared. By acknowledging it and how it challenges us to see it as it is, we can take baby steps to integrate it into our systems. We can invite open conversations on how we may transmute the situation to reframe, reimagine and rejuvenate our systems instead. How we perceive is going to determine the outcomes we invest in. If we see people and our resources as limited, we will stay limited in our approach and outcomes. We are unlikely to be risk-takers and might have a wait-and-see attitude. This could be okay for the interim. However, as 2030 draws close with our grandiose global commitments to limit and curtail carbon emissions and nature and biodiversity loss, stakeholder capitalism is our impending future. How we manage it now matters. Building trust so that our stakeholders can be assured of our quality of service or product matters.

This is why safety is an integral part of reputation management. Showing we care to provide for and ensure homes, workplaces, and countries are physically and psychologically safe for people to work, live, and play in raises people's confidence in co-existing with its many laws and requirements in exchange for peace of mind. This peace as we know it deep down cannot be understated as international collaboration and coalition building is only a thing of the recent past; before the Cold War, we were still largely a war-torn planet. We must do our best to safeguard and bring on our respective intelligence to work together for a co-prosperous world.

Safety involves addressing specific risks and implementing measures to mitigate those risks in each industry. Building trust and reliability involves adhering to safety standards and maintaining transparency, responsiveness, and a commitment to continuous improvement in safety practices. Safety is, therefore, crucial across various industries, and its definition often depends on the underwriting and operational and strategic risks unique to each sector. What we understand about safety at an individual level similarly translates to the systems level. Most importantly, how we relate to authority regarding safety management and related governance mechanisms, such as risk and compliance processes, is where it counts.

If authority figures made us feel somewhat (insert emotion of choice) when we were younger for (insert) reason, we would similarly act out these tendencies in our adult behaviour. The danger lies in seeming outwardly compliant but internally defiant. This is where we must nurture open, autonomous, and safe spaces for people to show up, build trust and take responsibility for their actions. Workplace cultures that support open communications would also respect our boundaries with space for negotiation should a boundary be too rigid.

Team reporting structures within respective workflows and at the overall organisational level are crucial. This allows respective stakeholders to contribute accordingly without second-guessing whether their efforts will be duplicative, rejected, or recognised. It is best to co-create the structures in consultation with as much transparency as possible. Remote work or hybrid working situations also call for such clarity to ensure accountability on the part of team members.

Most importantly, while success in key performance indicators is important for client-focused projects and/or revenue-focused businesses, sustainable businesses cultivate a culture of acceptance and flexibility if something does not go as planned. This may look like allocating buffer budgets in case of overshooting, considering new partners if manpower shortages occur, and promoting innovation within organisations to grow new product/service possibilities. The less performative we are about our performance indicators, the better our outcomes will be since we will be focused on what value was created for whom and when. This will help us be kinder to ourselves when faced with certain challenges (e.g., competitive work environments where information flow is limited as people protect their data to avoid another from 'knowing' for whatever reasons).

Organisations could delegate more to test the resiliency of their people when it comes to personal safety:

- How able are we to understand safety?

- Are there any struggles with attention to detail, such as following through with information?

- How may we place reminders or provide accessibility to information during high-stress situations?

Safety is a cornerstone of every industry. It is essential for protecting individuals and fostering trust, even as its emphasis varies across sectors and stakeholders. Whether in healthcare, aerospace, automotive, consumer products, food and beverage, construction, or technology, the commitment to safety shapes the experience and confidence of all stakeholders involved.

In the medical sector, safety is fundamentally about safeguarding patients from harm during care. This involves preventing medical errors, properly administering treatments, and protecting against infections. Key aspects include clinical safety, which ensures accurate diagnoses and effective treatments, and infection control, which minimises the risk of contagion. Patient privacy also plays a vital role, as protecting sensitive information fosters trust. Transparency in error reporting and adherence to evidence-based practices contribute to a culture of continuous improvement, reassuring patients that their well-being is the top priority.

On the other hand, aerospace safety centres on the aircraft's meticulous design, maintenance, and operation to prevent accidents. This includes rigorous engineering standards that guarantee mechanical reliability and operational protocols that train pilots and manage emergency situations. Trust in aerospace comes from a steadfast commitment to high safety standards and transparency regarding safety records, which is essential for maintaining public confidence in air travel.

In the automotive industry, safety encompasses vehicle design and manufacture to protect passengers and pedestrians. Features like airbags and anti-lock braking systems are critical, as is compliance with established safety standards. Effective recall management and clear communication about safety features help build consumer trust, emphasising the industry's dedication to passenger safety.

In the Fast-Moving Consumer Goods (FCMG) sector, safety means ensuring products are designed and manufactured to prevent user harm. This involves rigorous testing, quality control, clear labelling, and effective recall processes. Adherence to safety standards is crucial for fostering trust among consumers, especially if they rely on these products for everyday use.

Safety in the food and beverage sector revolves around delivering products free from contaminants and ensuring that the nutrition information disclosed is as accurate as possible. Hygienic food preparation, storage practices, and traceability are paramount to safeguarding public health. Companies can cultivate consumer confidence regarding their products by being transparent about sourcing and handling and promptly addressing safety issues. With cheaper supply chains and easier fabrication of authenticated products, consumers must be proactive in purchasing without taking any information for granted. Thankfully, with the advent of customer reviews and forums, consumers have more opportunities to gain assurance of products they wish to purchase.

Many people in developed building sectors do not consider construction safety thanks to the more strenuous regulations and requirements to ensure up-to-date building codes. However, safety lapses still occur for many reasons, and it is important to stay vigilant and aware at all times, even if we are passing by a construction site. Good developers emphasise construction safety, protecting workers and the public from the inherent hazards of development projects. This includes implementing robust safety measures within construction sites that monitor site operations' Environmental, Health, and Safety aspects and adherence to regulatory standards. A commitment to regular safety training and transparent incident reporting is necessary for safety ownership and building external stakeholder trust (specifically those who do not work on-site). Overall, this signals that we prioritise the well-being of our workers when addressing safety measures.

The least tangible safety consideration up till recently has been our data. As of 2024, we have been witnessing greater occurrences of scams globally and security breaches in our systems. Organisations prioritising strong data management and cybersecurity procedures implement robust measures to guard against breaches and ensure system reliability under expected and, ideally, unexpected conditions. This is necessary to build end-user trust. Most of us like to connect digitally without overthinking about the backend. We want to be assured that our digital assets are secure when transacting with collateral such as money or sensitive business information.

While the emphasis on safety may differ across industries, the underlying principle remains the same: safety is paramount. By prioritising safety, we understand that every scope of work comes with risks, stakeholder needs, and system limitations. Safety as a shared responsibility calls for us to foster trust with one another, report issues in time, and co-create solutions that close gaps.

Once trust is gone, it is difficult to earn it back.

It is easy to embrace our fears more these days with what is happening around us. How, then, may we feel safe as ourselves? Equity is difficult to understand as it varies based on stakeholders' interpretations of the system and its operation. Bridging any visible gap will require much more thinking, planning, and execution. Thinking about our perspectives before engaging others in a change initiative is helpful. Suppose we return to the earlier half of the chapter, where we discuss what makes us safe and how we may feel free from others in the previous chapter. In that case, we may understand how others need this and how to bring this sense of nuanced security into our existing systems to make them antifragile.

This is where the need to go inward will be important for leaders:

- What is it about equity that is known and unknown to us?

  _____

  _____

- How can we create accessibility with what we have?

  _____

  _____

- What would the best possible equitable set-up look like for us within our current set-up?

  _____

  _____

The outcomes of these successful measures will depend on our *consistency, commitment and courage levels*. Not everyone will be accepting of feedback; most of us shun our dark side, much less allow someone to tell us if there is something we need to do about it. The more we realise how it can help us grow as individuals, the *quicker this transformative age can occur*.

Understanding interdependence can help make it easier to understand why different people need to be included for co-creation to happen. Let's take the example of a simple cake shop. We have a family business, and everyone has a fixed role. They know what happens when an order comes in and who does what. However, a crisis almost always occurs when one member has to be out on leave or away for a delivery. How do we step in and ensure systems still run smoothly if we all have our own fixed roles? A more diverse setup where we train teams to understand each other's roles (to help and not take over someone's job) is more beneficial.

In this case, everyone knows what to do when a crisis happens. However, the buy-in and ownership for diverse setups to work depend on the visibility and recognition factors and culture, enabling transparent and fair distribution of work. Grudges and resentment over an unfair workload might arise in a family business set-up. However, work still gets done because everyone wants the business and their family name to succeed (with a few exceptions). Hence, for regular teams where members are not related, which is the case with most businesses and organisations, we need to create a safe space for everyone to perform their professional best and be fairly compensated through recognition and distribution of work.

If someone is highly skilled at something, ensuring others understand the value of that skill is important. If someone lacks knowledge or exposure, offering training to bring them on par is necessary. Helping them understand this training will then help them advance, and following through by supporting them will help build trust and loyalty in the organisation. Where a team member might be struggling (emotionally, mentally, physically) – having an honest conversation to meet them where they are at is important. Upon hearing about their self-disclosure, assessing what to do to support their productivity at the workplace will be necessary. Not addressing one member's issues often affects the team's morale.

In making self-awareness our primary goal, we remove any emotional charge from reminding ourselves of our weaknesses and how to manage them with others. We meet and forgive ourselves simultaneously, a crucial daily skill set. None of us are perfect, regardless of experience, knowledge or skill sets. In fact, given the transitions we are in, we all must keep growing, including leaders. Staying humble about this fact will be the first key to our success. This is followed by ensuring we constantly strive to be self-aware and show up better for ourselves and others around us. Thirdly, prioritise safe open spaces for everyone to offer unique abilities to ensure we can all come together to produce a robust output.

As leaders, we often take our team's feedback at face value because we lack the bandwidth to hold space or feel overwhelmed. There is also this perception that there are 'better things to do' than to babysit or manage an interpersonal issue between team members. If we commit most of our time to work, it would be beneficial to make it as pleasant as possible. Ensuring all conflicts are addressed promptly and having a culture of reciprocity practised openly helps the team mature into professional setups if they were not in the first place. Here culture of reciprocity refers to reminding our teams that helping and returning the favour are two important aspects of successful collaboration.

Anyone who seems overly dependent on others to help with their workload without offering the same assistance could be flagged for a growth discussion. A growth discussion ensures there is no fear in approaching this feedback session. The supervisor points out growth areas so that colleagues can understand the challenges their current behaviour presents and how they propose to manage it to make the workplace more harmonious.

We are all awakening to a quiet realisation of this need for integration in our hearts. Many of us are answering the call to embrace our shadow side as it appears more at the fore of how we are with ourselves and others. The difficult, hard-on-ourselves rhetoric and constant go-go-go feeling are becoming tiresome for most of us. We are feeling its effects wear us out. We are retreating to kinder, self-love practices that remind us to be gentle with ourselves. As leaders, recognising these trends and how our teams are evolving also matters. As cyclical beings of nature, we will not always be up and ready to go. When it is crunch time, we can communicate our expectations for all of us to be so, with much more room for compassion and flexibility, as not all of us can perform when told any longer.

Like a snake, we need time to shed the old skin, and when we or our teams or family members undergo this, let us hold space for them. Let them know we are here. While we wish for them to perform and be their 'old self', we must grieve that this is no longer to be. A new version is emerging, which needs to be renegotiated. Therefore, more frequent trust-building conversations where we meet each other will be needed. We all want to thrive. We sincerely do. Some days, we struggle with it and no longer wish to perform. Something more authentic is making its way through for us to show up as we are meant to, and as leaders, we need to allow that to happen as long as the job gets done.

As we work on our consciousness through self-awareness and it expands, we will notice that we may have been rigid and self-limiting in many ways, from how and what we think of ourselves and others to our perception of material and immaterial things. This is often the result of our upbringing and socialisation. We are made to think, act and feel in certain ways that 'worked out' for previous generations. When we decondition, we realise these models are still fear-based unless we are privileged to be born into enlightened families. These fear-based models teach us primarily to fear living, which is why we live constricted, restricted definitions of our lives based on fixed models of success. We dare not venture out of this silo because, truthfully, no one else might have or we do not know how.

When exposed to worlds outside what we know, we almost feel 'cheated' of staying stuck. We often fail to see how we dissociate, ignoring new possibilities and staying unhappy in one place. This happens when we limit our consciousness with self-doubt and worry. We get into a defensive and protective mode. We judge everything according to a certain lens and trust no one or thing, including ourselves, even if we think we do. We prefer holding on to the safety rails or blankets we have conjured over the years to stay 'safe'. This cocoons us until a certain point when we have to shift, evolve and grow for our highest good.

We pivot from such thinking as it has kept us in a box. We remember that constant and consistent evolution helps us realise our unlimited abilities and, most importantly, live freely. Many of us are happy to stay in our comfort zones because we may not know how to soothe ourselves or parent ourselves to new experiences that challenge and make us grow. We may believe this is our only lot in life; therefore, we 'deserve' this. Or this is for someone else to do, not me. Such energetic imprints in our DNA or energy field have existed for generations. It is what has made our ancestors feel helpless, hopeless and small within the context of many great upheavals and difficulties in human history. Their emotional experiences further entrench these painful untruths in our psyche until we start working to unearth the origin and realise the latent opportunities to connect with our true selves again.

The good news is that significant groundbreaking change does not happen overnight unless a catastrophe or windfall occurs. Such change often occurs gradually over time as we set our intentions to grow our consciousness. To disregard evolving would be to stay in whatever state of being we are in when we can be open and flow with the changes emerging to higher states of alignment with what we are here to be and do on Earth. It will be useful to reframe what a challenge or challenging energy is to us. For most of us, challenges are perceived as roadblocks. This can either be a demoralising feeling or a moment to pause. By this stage in the book, we are aware of our abilities to shift our reality to higher timelines by processing our emotional and mental blockages through the exercises shared. When we do this, we unlock another key to our consciousness and allow more light to enter to heal and enlighten us about what we truly want.

The *immature* masculine energy side of us would have us force through and make a hole through the challenging energy at the possibility of *burning out*.

The mature masculine energy knows to be patient and to assess the situation with a bit more due diligence – is this truly the most favourable route forward that will serve me and all around me? When our energy is affected by lower morale, for instance, it impacts our loved ones the most since we spend time with them regularly. We want to keep our energy levels balanced and relatively high so that we do not unassumingly take in other people's energies because we are too preoccupied to notice. Over time, this mindfulness and energy hygiene level can avoid low feelings of stagnation and help us move closer to realising our dreams. We are social beings, and mindfulness helps us stay connected and aware.

Next, challenges can also be interpreted as a test to reflect on what we want and where we could reprioritise if needed. It could also show us our passions in this space and whether we want to proceed. Again, the immature masculine energy would have us think we need to stick to something no matter what, especially if it is challenging, as this is a mark of a "strong" person, etc. There is a fine line between commitment and compulsion. A commitment that serves our highest good will bring breakthrough energy, and we will keep moving forward as long as this energy presents itself. However, to keep going forward when other parts of our lives fall apart will be compulsive. We can let go of this and hone the mature masculine energy of restoration instead.

How may we restore what we find lacking externally, inwardly instead?

Lastly, challenge energy can also be reframed as a growth opportunity to mature. How may we proceed forward without harm to ourselves and others? This is where spiritual evolution by raising our consciousness can present us with more beneficial options for our well-being – 1) does it help us achieve our goals? 2) what are the trade-offs (if any)? 3) is there an urgency in addressing this right now? 4) If yes, what scenario most likely affects our well-being? 5) If it is not urgent, what can we do in the interim to address this challenge with more resources, etc., in the future?

As the word suggests, maturity takes time, and we can use our retrospective life lessons and reflections to keep honing it.

From a divine feminine perspective, maturity presents itself when we can nurture environments within and around us to hold space and provide a sense of deep knowing that we are safe. This requires our intuitive sensemaking skills to go hand in hand with the logical thinking flow of the divine masculine. It will allow us to see situations as they are and how best we can move forward. For safety, intuition is perhaps the most neglected aspect of our being. We always need a tangible explanation or justification. However, as we spiritually evolve, our intuition will be instrumental because keeping order as we once knew it is not as easy. Globalised markets, independent variables of change everywhere, and unpredictable bad actors call for unprecedented reliance on ourselves to discern and make improved decisions for our and the collective well-being.

Making realistic adjustments in our systems will stem from knowing our competency, growth potential limitations and how we will work around them. Like challenge energy, limitations allow us to be grounded and work with what we have. It helps us appreciate the co-creative journey we must partake in with creative intelligence to move to the next level. As we give in to flow with the universal flow of resistance, synchronicity and gentle pauses or abrupt disruptions, we hone a deep state of humility, surrender and patience. We must slow down, rush less and breathe more frequently and deeper to stay connected with our inner guide. We can help our nervous systems cope by tending to their needs without having them constantly overworked. Overall, these experiences will help us realise a deep compassion towards ourselves regarding what we are going through and what we will be going through. It is not personal. It just is.

Hence, reaching co-prosperity requires this deep trust within ourselves to notice where we can plug the safety gaps within and around us. When we are safe, our outer world is safe. We can build from a place of love, hope and kindness, knowing all beings can be safe. We no longer need old stories of lack, pain and suffering. We start weaving new opportunities and synchronicities to recharge and revitalise ourselves and others. This begins with just one step forward daily, and it is safe to pause occasionally. In this chapter, we explore the element of fire to transform what no longer serves us into new life force energy, enabling us to move forward. Fire is a vital ally in construction, manufacturing, and cooking; without its heat and transformative power, we would not have our modern gadgets, food, or buildings. Moving forward, reconnecting with this primordial energy and acknowledging all that fire has provided and continues to offer is reverence in practice.

We can tune ourselves to the sound syllable of "Da", which has a low, rhythmic tone similar to the Schumann resonance, often called Earth's heartbeat. It can help us resonate with our ancestral connections to the land and listen to receive what we need. Nature, like safety, requires us to slow down and be more mindful of what is around us and what is happening to us. When we rush, we tend to look past important details, jump to conclusions, and have expectations that might not happen, causing further resentment, for instance. When we return to balance, we understand sustenance. This quality of what we truly need to live on Earth. Most times, it is not more money or material possessions but a deeper connection with oneself, especially in these challenging times of false hope through mass marketing, false prophets through ease and accessibility of transmitting messages online, as well as false securities in the stop-gap mechanisms we are developing to cope with our existing systemic challenges.

Safety emerges from trust, which is required firstly within ourselves. When we trust ourselves, we avoid creating further chaos for ourselves and others. We seek resonance with others rather than seeding discord and ensure we are always aware of where our solutions and measures fall short of safeguarding ourselves from risks. We are connected and ensuring our nervous systems are not on constant overdrive. We take responsibility for our anxieties and manage ourselves well before we manage others. Leaders, too, need to put the oxygen masks on themselves first before 'fighting fires'. We are all on unique timelines and pathways. Heading towards a unified direction requires us to flow with universal intelligence. Any time this shows up in plateau energy turning into a comfort zone, we know we are ready to change again. We will feel less anxious as we proceed because we will take the necessary action to care for ourselves and keep growing. Any energy of avoidance or procrastination is simply a coping mechanism we will soon realise we need to let go of if we wish to flow.

As described in various real-world applications above, safety is about getting out of harm's way, ensuring due processes, and following through on actions required to establish order over chaos. This is no different for our personal lives. When we show up for ourselves like this, we assure our inner world that we are safe, which projects a secure external world for us to live in. This is growing increasingly important in a fast-changing digital world.

V

REINSTATE COMMUNITY

I n 2024, the United Nations introduced the new '*Global Principles for Information Integrity*' to address critical challenges related to misinformation and disinformation. The principles emphasise the need for transparency, protection of human rights, and limitations on algorithmic control over information access.[28] The rise of misinformation is particularly concerning in the context of open-sourced artificial intelligence (AI). As highlighted by a report from Freedom House, generative AI is increasingly being exploited to create and disseminate false information, including fake news and deep fakes, which can manipulate public opinion and undermine trust.[29] The US Deputy Attorney General

---

[28] V. Mishra, UN News, 'Algorithms should not control what people see, UN chief says, launching Global Principles for Information Integrity', 24 June 2024, https://news.un.org/en/story/2024/06/1151376 (Accessed 12 September 2024).

[29] *Freedom on the Net, scores and ranks countries according to their relative degree of internet freedom, as measured by a host of factors like internet shutdowns, laws limiting online expression, and retaliation for online speech. The 2023 edition, released on October 4, found that global internet freedom declined for the 13th consecutive year, driven in part by the proliferation of artificial intelligence.* C. Gordon and B. Wheeler, BBC News, AI could 'supercharge' election disinformation, US tells the BBC', 15 February 2024, https://www.bbc.com/news/world-68295845 (Accessed 12 September 2024).

has warned that AI can significantly amplify disinformation, raising the potential for inciting violence and illustrating AI's complex, dual-edged nature in today's information landscape.[30] In response to these challenges, major tech companies like Meta, Google, and TikTok have committed to reducing misleading AI-generated content, particularly to safeguard the integrity of the upcoming 2024 US elections.[31]

The only antidote to these frightening trends will be building community resilience. Where we will be unlikely to tell reality from illusion, we can lean on one another to share real-time information after ensuring we have completed our due diligence. We will tap into our collective intelligence streams before we resort to manufactured information. Our intuition will play a bigger role in guiding us, and we inherently trust one another because we believe in not harming another. From knowing what information is ours to share, these values, principles and ethical code of conduct will be integral in communicating true intent. We are focused on what we need to know with adequate exposure to new information without feeling overwhelmed or afraid that we are missing out. We are grounded in mutualism, which helps us operate from safe, secure agendas rather than desperate and selfish ones.

Further, as we individually pursue pathways of authentic living, bliss consciousness, and transformation, as mentioned in the first half of this book, we create unified pathways towards one another. This creates a field of resonance stronger than our minds can understand. Here, social cohesion exists despite the diversity of identities simply because we believe we belong to ourselves and give ourselves the recognition we need.

Communities built from these individuals coming together are interdependent and focused on co-creating new value from true wealth perspectives. Naturally, our pathways aligned with living in nature can scale up and multiply at the community level. Mis/disinformation will be harder to spread in this resonance field as we trust each other to respect boundaries and ensure fear-mongering ends. We authenticate every piece of information with proper due diligence instead of knee-jerk reactions

[30]   Gordon and Wheeler, BBC News, AI could 'supercharge' election disinformation, US tells the BBC'.

[31]   Gordon and Wheeler, BBC News, AI could 'supercharge' election disinformation, US tells the BBC'.

from emotions or fear-based thinking. This element of looking out for each other, sharing accurate and relevant information, and building support systems and safeguards from bad actors during times of crisis will make all the difference.

These are not new concepts or ways of being. Close-knit communities, immigrant households, and minority groups have been practising these ways to achieve varying levels of co-prosperity. These groups understand the power of supporting each other in times of need in a reciprocal manner. By helping a new immigrant settle in, for instance, an instantaneous gratitude bond is established. This is especially true when help is least expected, particularly from a stranger. If offered in a non-binding way, this creates a powerful resonance field of reciprocity where the receiver is more likely to offer help back or pay it forward. When we scale these efforts through a multiplier effect, our societies' cultures and social norms inherently shift for the better. This is where trust can organically emerge to safeguard humanity from ourselves. This only works if the receiver is not entitled to help or obliged to return any favours. It works when we are willing and able to give and receive. Any other energy thought forms will distort this pure resonance field.

'Having co-prosperity as a value can help us strengthen the practice of our own and others' dignity'.[32]

Built on reciprocity, these communities will be largely non-transactional and values-driven. People look out for one another based on the value of co-prosperity. They understand the struggles the other has faced and share their resources for a time when they may need the favour back. This has been witnessed in many instances of crowdfunding, where micro-loans are extended to community members to tide them over their difficult period in life thanks to the pooling of resources by other community members. This mutual understanding of specific lived realities makes the experiences of being part of a community more meaningful than living an isolated existence where one could be more vulnerable. Trust builds further when

---

[32] D. Kaur, 'The Action Gap: Business Strategies for Co-Prosperity', 2024, Partridge, p.96.

we allow safe spaces for authentic expressions of our lived experiences to be shared. This is why groups with similar backgrounds or experiences understand each other better. From this mutual understanding, there is more room to foster trust-building when we practice active listening and respect for each other's boundaries. When we know what information is ours to share, we no longer rely on unhealthy bonding methods of gossiping to build relationships. Instead, we shift into holding space and allowing community members to grow by offering new opportunities for co-prosperity across different realms of our lives – from our identities to value creation.

So often, we might believe systems are at fault for their lack of fairness, impartiality, transparency, and due process until new solutions emerge from bottom-up communities focused on bridging the gaps. Our systems' inequities inevitably birth these parallel social movements that promote accessibility in order not to leave anyone behind. Accessibility to information via advocacy groups, accessibility to daily needs via charity organisations and accessibility to humanitarian aid via non-profits. Perhaps this is how Nature works as well. Offshoots from primary rainforests allow ecosystems to develop around them, bringing in other hosts, such as animal, insect, and plant species, to make the system whole. How beautiful is that? These informal support structures through our self-help communities are often leaner, more agile and less bureaucratic in aid. With such a reframe, we might perhaps appreciate the dysfunctions in our collective systems and think about syncing the informal with the formal in a closed-loop web so that no one else falls through.

This requires identifying the need for co-living, co-existence and cooperation. Given the narratives of our family lines, we can either be closed off to support systems or lead them ourselves. Often, we are closed off when we have been hurt by another, unable to trust someone or unwilling to receive out of shame, guilt or embarrassment. Noticing which of these apply to us can help us unpack our shadow stories and heal them with self-compassion and reconciliation. We are meant to be interdependent so that love can come through. We each have a unique offering. When we unify, we become more than the sum of parts, co-creating realities we would never have thought possible. For this to be realised, we need to heal. We must accept that we are not perfect, as are other people and our systems since we make them. And we do not have to stay flawed. We can rebuild better with mindful awareness and commitment to our growth journeys.

At its core, our systems have been progressively built on insurance and assurance ecosystems, revealing a fundamental trust gap. The insurance industry encourages us to take proactive steps to protect ourselves; otherwise, we risk facing unwanted hospital bills. It also prompts us to invest in our future now, given uncertainties like inflation that can devalue our savings. Similarly, the assurance industry reminds us that we cannot take financial or sustainability reports at face value and must seek third-party verification. There is an inherent flaw in the communications of these ecosystems. Are we unable to look after ourselves leading up to our death? From a grounded perspective, can we communicate that financial and non-financial reporting does not make or break a business, but the leadership attitudes and projected roadmaps to foster resilience matter more?

Understanding these connections between care, empathy, and solidarity from a rights-based approach is vital for all of us, particularly for business professionals and policymakers. By recognising the importance of trust in our systems, we can better embrace diversity and work toward creating more equitable and inclusive frameworks. This understanding is crucial in addressing deep-rooted structural injustices exacerbated by economic globalisation. While not everyone is on a level playing field, we can raise our consciousness through ongoing spiritual evolution to uncover our unique blueprints and show up to our fullest potential.

Solidaristic recognition acknowledges equal rights by understanding and responding to the unique circumstances of diverse groups.[33] It also goes beyond individual agency by requiring responsiveness and receptivity towards each other and our systems via care and empathy.[34] What each of us is doing and how it contributes to the whole becomes an integral movement towards healing the whole. We are okay with divisive opinions

---

[33] C.C. Gould, (2008). Recognition in Redistribution: Care and Diversity in Global Justice. *The Southern Journal of Philosophy Vol. XLVI*, p.100 http://www.carolcgould.com/uploads/1/2/5/0/12505497/published_article_recognition_in_redistribution.pdf

[34] Gould, Recognition in Redistribution: Care and Diversity in Global Justice, p.98.

and consensus. We can work towards a middle ground together. We can facilitate by holding space ingeniously and creatively through tools like visual storytelling. We understand if the hypocrisy of our actions plays out in our environments. There is no better way to build trust than to keep walking our talk with openness and transparency like water. If unclean, water can be filtered. Likewise, let us keep filtering our thoughts of dogma, ideologies and social conditioning that keep us feeling constricted. Let us flow with clarity, trusting that we are eternally safe because we are one with our environments and will have a solution for every roadblock or growth opportunity.

Telling stories that inspire us to take action and to remember who we are will be key now.

Since the dawn of civilisation, humans have instinctively organised and built communities. Today, forming virtual communities is more accessible than ever, thanks to platforms that facilitate networking, sharing of information, and marketing services or products from a hyperlocal to a global scale. More connected and established communities focus on mutual support for daily needs, where members earn a 'good' status by volunteering their time or expertise, thereby building credibility within the collective. This active participation strengthens the community and enhances each member's acknowledgement of what they can offer. Solidaristic recognition comes through when diverse individuals in groups feel heard, seen and acknowledged in ways where they are less reliant on identifying with a particular role in their life because they are assured of an authentic sense of belonging based on their interests or abilities. This strengthens the social good within the community, which can further expand at the societal level to bolster communal resilience. This is useful during challenging times, as providing safe spaces and growth opportunities within these communities allows people to contribute in non-traditional ways to feel good and supported. When more people are connected and feeling good, even the tough times seem manageable because we know we have each other.

Recognising these intrinsic benefits, the motivations behind engaging and building community must be thoughtfully considered to foster reciprocal relationships. To create meaningful connections, we must regulate our agendas consistently. In a truly reciprocal community, the value of what we offer cannot be measured in direct exchanges; rather, it lies in our commitment to be present for those who need support and to deliver our assistance when required. By doing so, we cultivate a space where everyone can negotiate and renegotiate their identities, fostering more profound understanding and collaboration. Table 7 below presents a simplified overview of contemporary communities, highlighting their potential to evolve into heart-centred, reciprocal environments that nurture trust.

Common Types of Community	Purpose	Benefit	Trust Factor
Owned by one person	Building a personal network to enrich one's own business/life mission	**Audited** as each entrant is vetted or personally connected with the network builder – this creates some resonance with the thematic focus of the community	It depends on *our responsiveness and receptivity* as members of these communities towards fellow members, shared content, and organised activities. Higher engagement may allude to higher levels of trust based on the requirements of our agendas. If our agenda is to create a network, we might engage more because we trust the quality of the people present and wish to build relationships with them.
Founded by one person, led by many others	To promote a shared goal that members resonate with and feel inclined to self-organise	**Autonomous,** spontaneous and diverse, depending on varying interests	
Part of an established entity	To build relationships and encourage regular engagements to create new value for members to keep growing	**Solidaristic** as it has a vested interest in keeping members engaged and curating relevant offerings for them, both from a top-down and bottom-up perspective	

Table 7: A simplistic overview of how we may organise ourselves these days based on our personal and professional interests

Resonance will be a key gel for most if not all, communities.

When we pay attention to specific cultural and social differences, we can construct suitable economic, social, and political institutions that do not advocate uniformity and support a range of conditions needed for well-being, especially safety, freedom, and fair, equitable access to participation. This is necessary in addressing structural injustices arising from economic globalisation. Here, the theories of Nancy Fraser and Axel Honneth offer complementary insights that can inform the practice of redistributive justice.[35]

Nancy Fraser advocates for a dual approach that intertwines recognition and economic redistribution. She argues that social justice requires acknowledging and respecting diverse identities and experiences and a fair distribution of resources and opportunities. This means that addressing cultural inequalities must go hand-in-hand with tackling economic disparities. Fraser's perspective emphasises that effective social justice must consider both the value of identity and the necessity of equitable resource allocation.

Conversely, Axel Honneth places recognition at the heart of his theory of justice. For Honneth, social justice is fundamentally about recognising and valuing individuals for their identities and contributions. He posits that achieving this recognition is crucial for personal dignity and social cohesion. While he emphasises the importance of recognition, Honneth's

---

[35]   Please note that the sources supporting my analysis of Fraser's and Honneth's works were contributed by ChatGPT, which I subsequently corroborated in my literature review. ChatGPT was utilised here to generate insights and summarise relevant concepts of redistribution and recognition, primarily from the following sources:

Thompson, S. (2005). Is redistribution a form of recognition? comments on the Fraser–Honneth debate. *Critical Review of International Social and Political Philosophy*, *8*(1), 85–102. https://doi.org/10.1080/1369823042000335876

N. Fraser and A. Honneth, *Redistribution or Recognition?: A Philosophical Exchange*, London and New York, Verso, 2003

N. Fraser, 'From Redistribution to Recognition? Dilemmas of Justice in a 'Post-Socialist' Age', in Anne Phillips (ed.), *Feminism And Politics: Oxford Readings In Feminism* (Oxford, 1998; online edn, Oxford Academic, 31 October. 2023), https://doi.org/10.1093/oso/9780198782063.003.0021, Accessed 10 October 2024

A.Honneth, *The Struggle for Recognition: The Moral Grammar of Social Conflicts*, Great Britain, Polity Press, 1995

framework can be somewhat narrower, focusing primarily on identity rather than the broader economic context.

Fraser's comprehensive approach becomes particularly relevant in redistributive justice, which seeks a fair allocation of resources to address inequalities. Key principles of redistributive justice include equity—distributing resources based on individuals' needs and contributions; prioritising assistance for those in greatest need; and responsibility—encouraging those with more resources to share with those who have less. This approach is often operationalised through policies like progressive taxation, social welfare programmes, and public services designed to reduce economic disparities.

By integrating Fraser's emphasis on recognition and redistribution with Honneth's focus on recognition's centrality, we can better understand how to address the structural injustices embedded in economic globalisation. A robust application of redistributive justice would seek to reallocate resources and foster an environment where diverse identities are acknowledged and respected, creating a more equitable and cohesive society. Thus, the real-world application of these theories can pave the way for a more just and inclusive global economic landscape.

We will need inclusive Economic policies that ensure equal access to education, healthcare, and employment to empower individuals and reduce inequality through a rights-based approach with equity enablers in place to level the playing field. This will look contextually different even across one economy, working collaboratively with relevant stakeholders to foster multi-stakeholder partnerships to understand the whole of a problem for clear and achievable long-term outcomes. Behavioural and mindset shifts are usually the first hurdle we must cross, as most of us are either benefactors of current systems or largely apathetic given the current state of affairs. New energy will be required to push through, and this is where ensuring that as many diverse people can sit at the decision-making table and share ownership will be instrumental.

Our focus will be rebuilding social protection floors where we can protect individuals from economic shocks to empower them to make the necessary shifts to stay afloat. Here, our welfare state policies and accompanying payouts must be revisited to ensure we are not building lethargy into our systems by de-incentivising our electorate from working in the economy. We will require objective data-sharing between recruitment and lending entities with government agencies to spot the red flags earlier with regards to gaps in job skills, retraining, upskilling and credit payment defaulting to sense where people might need help but are either unaware or got off guard with market trends of retrenchment or furlough. Our systems can be more robust, more intuitively built and self-learning once we understand why care, empathy, and solidarity are important in our communities.

Our intervention programmes also need a boost in the issues we seek to address in our communities. Innovative solutions require a very good understanding of what we are building – from a robot to software – and what purpose it needs to serve. Here, the purpose must go beyond building the Airbnb or Uber of something to unlock our potential to co-prosper truly. Redefining wealth will be the main normative shift we must make as we transition to such thinking. How much money is sufficient, and how can we use the rest of our time and resources to build solidaristic systems that will embed more trust and assure us of safer, greener and more co-creative futures? How may we move from highly vulnerable circumstances to feeling safe?

Community wealth has long depended on a few succeeding and contributing back, with little to no reciprocity.

Redefining wealth makes it accessible for all of us to attain true inner affluence and find the creative solutions needed to transcend our realities. By taking full responsibility, we heal our relationships, achieve balance, and foster harmony like bees do. Bees represent harmony, productivity, and divine direction. They show us how to be dedicated, focused, and industrious through focused work, as have many communities that have had to rebuild from disaster recovery, recession, and economic downturns. Their selfless cooperation to attain shared goals also shows that we can co-create a new value system for what it means to be a community.

Mining our inner worlds requires these exact qualities. This is where the potential for alchemy exists and true transformation to our higher potential. It requires self-acceptance of our shadow and light aspects and self-forgiveness towards ourselves and others as we uncover ways we have been dishonourable. Along with personal development, transformation, and spiritual advancement, we can further harness our talents to nurture our creative instincts. This requires a positive mindset, one that is open to begin with. It will also help to evaluate our agendas when we think of community:

Why am I part of or why have I created a community? What purpose does it fulfil?

What drives me to contribute to a community (i.e. my values, a higher vision, other people, etc)?

What motivates me to promote community-building (i.e., service mindset, social media presence, need for credibility/validation)?

What am I holding on to (i.e. old stories, inherited thought forms, etc)? How may I genuinely let go of my agenda (i.e. how may I engage at the same level with someone else with no expectations)?

How can I ensure information shared in the community is safe for all? What is my current due diligence process? How are we building trust?

These are not easy questions to answer as they may trigger memories or socialised lessons about how we need to perform to be considered a 'good' or 'respectable' person in society. Often, this makes us give more, leading to overextension of ourselves. It makes it difficult for us to receive. True giving comes from the heart and pure intentions. It has no expectations, and it aims at empowering others to succeed. If and when we notice resentment towards another building up or sheer fatigue, we will know we are off course somehow. That somewhere, we have taken on more than we can manage and need to rebalance. This brings us back to our values-based approach in life. How do we wish to co-prosper with others, and where can wealth (in material, body, mind and spirit sense) be used to entrench this concept?

Bees do this naturally. They co-exist in a community structure where everyone plays their role to benefit the whole. With this consciousness to co-create, they are the sole reason our flora and fauna thrive with their widespread pollination power and consistency. We 'enjoy' the honey they make as a by-product, often with little consideration to the efforts required to produce it until we reflect. How may we emulate this spirit and give back to nature? This is where our awakened potential, based on the same ethos, can be applied to develop solutions that emulate nature-based solutions that potentially solve ecological issues yet to emerge. To facilitate this transition, our institutional structures must evolve to promote unity over division, emphasising a values-based management approach. This shift will require prioritising sectors that benefit the collective rather than just a select few. We need to focus on meaningful financing outcomes, even if they may initially appear financially unfavourable by traditional standards.

Crucially, new systems must consider **double materiality**, ensuring that internal and external impacts of business operations and financial and non-financial factors are considered. This will involve leveraging robust technology to identify real-time needs and develop scalable, implementable solutions. Financing for these initiatives could derive from private capital created by avoided Economic, Governance, Social, Environmental, and Ethical (EGSEE) earnings, all supported by effective change management strategies and regenerative business models. The sooner we recalibrate how our business communities share information and best practices in building robust, sustainable, and circular business models, the quicker we can transition to a co-prosperous world where we can create new value for Nature instead of consistently taking what is finite.

As leaders[38] we can ask ourselves:

- ☐ Am I in tune with my inner world?
- ☐ Am I always mindful of my actions, thoughts and deeds
- ☐ Am I nourished?
- ☐ Do I walk the talk based on what I say?
- ☐ Do I accept and honour my past and 'weaknesses'?
- ☐ Am I aware of my shadow, gift and infinite potential?
- ☐ Do I give and receive in balance?
- ☐ Am I aligned with my highest expression of Truth?

As teams, we can ask ourselves:

- ☐ Am I in control of my responses to external stimuli?
- ☐ Am I aware of what is happening around me?
- ☐ Do I suspend judgement by practising compassion?
- ☐ Can I hold space for myself/others by building my patience?
- ☐ Can I let go of what I recognise is not within my control?
- ☐ Do I make choices for the highest good of everyone?
- ☐ Am I able to express my gratitude frequently?
- ☐ Can I stay connected with others to work things out together?

Aligning with this approach ensures we promote fundamental workplace values that include and are not exclusive to integrity, respect, accountability, teamwork, excellence, customer focus, adaptability, professionalism, communication and work-life balance. These values foster a positive work environment, encouraging employee motivation and

---

[36] *Please refer to 'The Action Gap: Business Strategies for Co-Prosperity' for additional resource on 'dignity® Audit' – this is a checklist of desired actions and corresponding state of wellness for leaders to consider when cultivating team culture and workflow progress to meet sustainable outcomes.*

contributing to overall organisational success and sustainability. Moreover, values act as an important moral compass to guide ethical decision-making. It builds trust, promotes cultural cohesion, supports personal growth and shapes individual and community behaviour towards a more just society.

What are some low-lying fruits we can implement to align with an EGSEE approach today:

☐ **Ask for feedback and ideas:** conduct stakeholder materiality assessments or any form of interviews with key stakeholders (off the record is better)

☐ **Organise group strategy sessions:** introduce this concept to fellow leaders and encourage a holistic approach to tackle the next business expansion plan or market outreach initiative

☐ **Update existing policies and guidance:** provide up-to-date information where ownership can be delegated to as diverse number of business unit representatives as possible

Knowing how industries work and how they may transition towards this New World will be our core problem statement.

The good news is that we create our systems. This means we can initiate change at the individual leadership level. We need to shift towards ethical conduct that emphasises responsible sourcing and extraction of resources. We must begin to use resources wisely to minimise negative downstream impacts. As leaders, we must recognise what is at stake and take action to drive necessary change. However, we might find ourselves overwhelmed by immediate concerns. To make room for important discussions about business transformation, we need to leverage the talent and institutional knowledge within our organisations, if we have not.

Figure 14: A model for healing workplace dynamics

By remembering the wisdom of bees, we can be inspired by the hive connectivity that brings an entire swarm of bees together to work in mutual harmony and agreement with the leadership. Referencing Figure 14,

o **Pause:** Am I feeling frustrated/tired/upset?
o **Reflect:** What has happened? How may we de-escalate a situation? Am I sharing information that is not mine to share? Where are we missing a fresh perspective?
o **Go:** Choose harmony; choose to give another the benefit of the doubt. Focus on maintaining our personal inner peace with mindful interactions and nurturing our teams to do the sale. We never really know what another person or colleague is undergoing, and they may be too fearful to be vulnerable with us. Holding space for them is sufficient, and when possible, open and safe spaces can allow for these conversations to take place so that adequate support can be provided. We all deserve to thrive and may not know how. As leaders, we can offer the right guidance for our teams.

This is where our systems will need to free themselves of others (e.g., bad actors), desires (e.g., power), and fear (e.g., anarchy) to usher in New World thinking that unite rather than divide so that we can all be absolved of the great suffering we have endured for generations. The future need not be bleak, and the power is in our hands to wield justice, harmony, and love. It is also time we all step away from our indifferent selves and master versatility to navigate these challenging times. Promising technologies such as free energy, bioenergetics, and renewable energy are available but waiting for patient capital to scale up. The moment our minds can open to receive what we have labelled as pseudo-science or disruptive financial instruments, the more lives we can save from impending climate refugee crises, food insecurities and potential social upheaval.

We are part of a whole. We need to think whole now.

Social cohesion grows when we feel safe enough to trust. We are assured of each other's interests so that we can support and grow together. We are not self-promoting or manipulative. However, we start disconnecting when the resonance frequency is one of taking rather than reciprocity. We are social beings wired to know this difference innately, which is why many of us are living in nuclear family units compared to more communal multi-generational family units where one family member can rely on another in times of need. What has happened with globalisation is personal greed has escalated due to the prevalence of opportunities. It has also bred corresponding reliance on those more prosperous among us to 'give back'. We isolate ourselves to escape being 'exploited' or 'dependent upon' by others. We form smaller groups that fit our purposes for a sense of community, which may be more self-serving than we like to acknowledge. Over time, this divide within society grows and seeds a deep discord that it takes just as long to heal.

We need to begin to heal now. *Where have we isolated ourselves, and why? What does community mean to us, and how may we reframe it to strengthen our contribution to social cohesion?*

Expanding our consciousness ensures we are as aware of our intentions as much as our actions. Follow-through will benefit the whole unit when a fellow community member seeks help. When someone feels supported in their times of need, we can ensure all of us succeed, thanks to the intangible energy exchange of gratitude. This will require us to shift from a transactional or 'what is in it for me' perspective to 'how may I contribute based on my bandwidth and what I have right now'. If we cannot give in terms of resources, that is ok – our positive and encouraging energy or presence is just as vital, if not more. New World economics will likely shift as we rebuild communities with heart-based leadership. Trust in our global ecosystem is weakening as we allow separatist sentiments and distorted Media frames to affect and influence our collective thought forms. Whether we know it or not, we are subtly affected by the will of the whole, so let us make sure to influence it positively. Where there might be green wishing, let us set realistic targets and adjust according to what we can do. Where there is greenwashing, let us ensure the actors are educated on the error of judgment on their end and allow them to make rectifications before litigation claims.

Wealth or survival is linked to our root chakra. When it is in balance, we neither hoard nor overspend. We are consciously aligned with our dharma and ensure we respond to the world around us in co-creative, dignified, and benevolent ways. We see the other as a fellow human with equal rights of access to opportunities and mobility. We are cognizant of staying grounded and ensuring we can continue supporting and contributing to our communities as we evolve.

A New World, New Earth, is a utopia on which we are awakened and risen to our respective challenges to bring online a more conscious way of living in sync with the momentums around us in a way that drives a passionate overhaul of what no longer works into new synergistic movements that uplift and restore our human spirit to the fore once again.

In this space-time continuum, we are proactively seeking our evolutionary progress for the betterment of all beings so that we may co-prosper within the 'limiting' realms to birth new realities that support higher timelines for all of us to expand our consciousness. Many of us are currently bogged down by limited bandwidth, a myriad of responsibilities, distractions, and social conditioning that we are overcoming in every moment. For those of us who do not see ourselves needing to work through this, you have either come on Earth with awakened minds or are blessed to know what needs to be our priority right now. Everything in balance requires us to be balanced as well. As multi-dimensional beings, we need our physical, emotional, spiritual, mental, interpersonal and community aspects to be on par. It does not matter how much we contribute to these different realms, but the effort to ensure we consider all aspects of our daily lives to stay balanced is more important. The financial and vocational alignment will come indirectly through this balanced alignment. Our natural gifts, known and unknown, will help us attract opportunities that are more aligned with how we are meant to serve.

Our possible future includes us knowing how full our tanks are across our multidimensional states of being (i.e., spiritual, mental, emotional, physical, interpersonal, and community). We will then show up better. We will be more fulfilled and aware and see things as they are. We will be as centred as we can be. We will no longer take ourselves for granted and receive the peace of knowing all is well regardless of what seems to be happening around us. We also recalibrate how we respect ourselves and others by upholding high standards of integrity in our thoughts, words and actions. In this evolutionary state, we harness the balance of our divine feminine and masculine energies to move forward intuitively along our *dharma*. We are mindful of what we absorb, communicate and achieve. We make constant amends to attune to the highest vibrational field of possibilities around us for our highest good and that of others. As we purify, we build more trust within ourselves and in life. Table 8 shows examples of how we can mend our hearts and relationships by choosing to reframe. We are together in this, one way or another.

Let's tell ourselves what we need to heal, evolve, and move on.

OPENING OUR HEARTS...	CHOOSING TO REFRAME...
I AM SORRY TO THOSE I HURT, ESPECIALLY MYSELF	*I deserve to treat myself with kindness. We deserve to treat ourselves with kindness.*
I ACCEPT MYSELF	*The inevitable truth is I am a peaceful, loving, and happy soul; let me be attuned to this.*
I ACCEPT MY SITUATION	*My blueprint is unique, and I am finding my way.*
I RELEASE EXPECTATIONS	*The universe has its timing to prepare us to be ready to receive what we need to level up.*
I LET GO OF WHAT NO LONGER SERVES ME	*Everything has had to happen; we can let go.*
I FORGIVE OTHERS	*Knowingly and unknowingly, we hurt each other, and I accept the role I play to know better next time.*
I FORGIVE MYSELF	*I see how I have harmed myself and do better next time.*
I LOVE MYSELF	*Let me tend to my inner garden, which deserves my undivided attention to flourish authentically.*
I LOVE OTHERS	*Unity consciousness allows me to hold space for another from a place of self-compassion.*
I TRUST LIFE	*This is life – the good and the bad. It is my school, and I am acknowledging its lessons.*
THANK YOU	*There is so much happening in the unseen; if only we knew.*

Table 8: To reach the eventual state of a co-prosperous world, we will embody the following sentiments from our genuine heart spaces thanks to the integration work we are embarking on through various mental and emotional healing presented in this book

We are here on Earth to be sustained by the abundant energetic flows available when we walk on the soil, take deep breaths and watch the waves roll forward towards us. These sights, sounds, smells and touch activate our multi-sensory self to come alive and ensure our inner energetic field is intact and strengthened by pure energy that knows no side and is replenishing and recharging. Understanding our unique human bodies and energetic fields means we must be more mindful of our boundaries across our multi-dimensional field. This need not alarm or scare us. Instead, we must take ownership and inform others of our needs to help us stay well-regulated, safe, secure, and trustworthy. Table 9 depicts the unhealthy constructs of boundaries within our social settings that need transmuting for us to realise co-prosperity.

BOUNDARIES

SOCIALLY ACCEPTED BUT HARMFUL TO US	Uncommon or not socially accepted
LISTEN TO PEOPLE'S RANTS	Stating you are not comfortable or at a bandwidth to engage/receive/listen
COMMENT	Holding space
OFFER UNSOLICITED ADVICE, SOLUTIONS	To say we only want someone to listen or we do not know what to say
EXTEND SYMPATHY, PITY	Empathy (i.e. "I understand where you are coming from"

*Table 9: How we can inform others of what is
not socially common or acceptable yet*

In the New World, we are all given rehabilitative chances to make our dreams of a united world come true. It is not idealistic if we know how ancient civilisations, much more complex and sophisticated than ours, have existed on this principle of co-prosperity. When we remember the past within each of us, activating our consciousness to raise our vibration will be our first step.

With every investment we make in purifying our bodies, emotions, minds, and souls, we will help the collective rise up.

There are many of us doing this work in all corners of the world without the need for recognition or acknowledgement. Every morning, in every corner of the world, we have initiates meditating, contemplating, and bringing the new consciousness within themselves and their environments online. We, too, can get started, and we need not wait until we are retiring, when we have a crisis, or when we have more time. We are self-healing, and the effects are multiplied when we come together in a community to heal. We build solidaristic ties bound by our shared pain and common experiences. When we believe this, our external realities shift to accommodate more authentic connections with others where we can be ourselves. We then build truthful realities because we understand where our pain and the pain of others come from. We no longer hide in self-pity or shame and notice when another does to help them emerge out of their shells. We are self-aware to avoid re-victimisation and ensure dignity for ourselves and others. This amplifies in a community when we can relate to what is happening within and among us.

We can co-create new ways of being with one another that allow for our shedding and blossoming simultaneously.

Communities that have the responsibility to act emerge as a result. We are no longer bystanders or isolating ourselves and others. We offer a hand or two and relate on an empathic level like never before. We maintain our boundaries, especially in ensuring our energetic centres are balanced. Instead of depending on one another for solutions, we can co-create new outcomes based on our strengths. We build interdependent systems where our value correlates with others to create true wealth. This has been seen in the example of the shared economy, where community members share a resource without committing to high financial investments. The accessibility to a product or service that was once too expensive helps others be more productive with their time or gain a new skill that eventually creates win-win outcomes for all. More virtuous loops support further proliferation of communities with a responsibility to act, which will contribute to overall co-prosperity. The magic is already happening.

So, let us make the quantum leaps to align our desires with our vibrating thoughts and emotions towards unity consciousness. As we relentlessly pursue this inner harmony, it inevitably creates a synarchy outside of ourselves through our way of being. We no longer get caught between two worlds as our fields of resonance unify with singularity. This is where synchronicities occur spontaneously as our *dharma* unfolds. We can take one step closer to happiness in each moment. This is when we *transcend the fear frequencies* to bring expedited healing online for ourselves and others by showing them it is safe.

The only challenge is taking the first step, specifically into the unknown and being continuously led by our inner guide. We have the blueprint for our authentic happiness within us. The fear of going inward to uncover this blueprint results from conditioning and programming, making us think we will not be safe. This must be uprooted, and we must do it our way. When we are connected with our Higher Self, we will be guided lovingly towards growth and expansion, which will always be safe. Should we indulge in self-destructive or impulsive measures, please note that there is a dynamic coming up that needs to be healed. There is always time, and growth is not meant to physically or emotionally harm us. Our ego-mind will retaliate, and we can overcome the mental stress of rising confusion and lack of clarity by focusing on our breathing. What we need in every moment is available when we return to the present. The past no longer applies, and the future has yet to be. We are now choosing the highest timeline and vibration for ourselves that can shift everything beyond our imagination. The more we do this, the more we ascend beyond what we once thought possible. We must do the inner work; there are no shortcuts.

When we ascend and clear these imprints of fear, we rise to new levels of being that may seem challenging until we overcome them. What we think, do and say during the liminal state of change between growth spurts factors into our newer attitudes and perceptions of the 'challenge' at hand. Will it cause us undue stress from overthinking, rumination, and doomsday thinking, or will we hold space for ourselves when a change occurs to tell ourselves we will be okay? The possible guilt or fear for stepping out of our comfort zone is not ours. We are ever-evolving and can venture into the unknown responsibly; it is what we are here to do. Any time we feel lost is a sign of our divine masculine energy needing attention – where have we been too hard on ourselves, what have we allowed ourselves to get carried away with, and how may we re-centre? It is also a sign to allow our divine feminine to lead the way with our presencing of change occurring within and around us through our intuitive abilities. We are change beings at our core; let us return to our true nature.

The notions of responsibility may be tricky here. How may we safely evolve with our modern-day responsibilities, which include mortgage payments, family and care duties, and job requirements? All this sounds like too much work that requires us to allocate time and appropriate spaces to contemplate and embody.

The universal flow is kind. It does not deliberately uproot us unless we have been stagnant for too long and are unwilling to move forward for many reasons. Otherwise, we are evolving daily, and the more attuned we are to the flow of our life in the temporal dimension, the quicker we realise that we must give in to this power without letting our minds create diseases for us. When something unexpected occurs, we may naturally get frustrated and act out. This is the immature divine masculine aspect in us that thinks we have full control and things should always go as expected. Life and situations are not personal. There is a divine flow that ensures what needs to happen happens for us to learn the lessons we need to keep purifying our essence and levelling up.

When similar situations keep recurring, we can question how much we have understood what is unfolding before us and how we may effectively move forward – this need not mean a drastic change in our jobs or living situations. Often, a reframe in thinking is all we need to reset the energy charge behind situations to see it from a new light or fresh perspective without judging it. When we resent, hold on to revenge energy and allow our ego-mind to guide our actions, we tend to take 'drastic' action. Nevertheless, often drastic action, whether well-considered or not, can also lead to great evolutionary change as we dislodge ourselves to fully consider the impacts of our decisions and how it has impacted the people around us and ourselves. Like Nature, we can ebb and flow with its ways and sync ourselves to its cycles of change to succeed. Such wisdom is hard to come by but is present in the many written works of our early philosophers, poets, political thinkers and even playwrights.

As seasons change, how do we show up even in our urban or tropical lives where the weather and diets may not change as much?

The potential for future communities lies deep within us as we birth new collective ways of being in union with ourselves and others. The thriving communities of our future are built on the belief that we are guided at all times and that everything is occurring for our highest good. We can have what is most beneficial and necessary for us now, even if it is not what we want. In hindsight, it would be what we needed to transform and experience authentic joy. The resultant energies are multi-fold: expansive, grounded and blissful. We are free of our safety clutches that offer false comforts and walking independently onward to co-create new realities and timelines for ourselves and everyone around us. We respect the path and unfolding needed for each member, and we support each other by sharing stories and space.

In future communities, we slow down to centre ourselves and build resonance with one another. We trust our life force to guide us in our growth journeys, and we accept the perceived pain as a blessing for our eventual state of mind and being. We are one hundred per cent committed to staying in our relationships through learning and evolution. We always remind ourselves and others to keep our hearts open, feeling each other's presence in every moment and tuning in to visions of higher potential for one another. We are united, we are flow itself, and we become devoted.

The road to inner freedom has no right or wrong pathways, and neither pain nor happiness is slated. It simply is. When we overcome the difficulty of opening ourselves and being fully present in a moment or experience, we naturally accept and nurture a safe holding space within us that we will be ok. We take each step forward and only look back to see how far we have come.

Progress in our future communities will be collective ascension. We are all connected, and when one of us suffers, we know they will emerge out of it to meet us where we are as we hold space for ourselves. When life gets hard, we will be required to unlearn the addictive patterns of repressing ourselves and reacting to situations. Our only response would be, "How can I take the next step forward?" The responsibility to act will come from many experiences of collective grieving as the life we once knew will transition to greener, safer and more inclusive societies. This harmonisation in our new norms will likely be 'scary' to a few of us because we are habituated to our dualistic interpretations of life. Let us be assured that we are headed on a positive trajectory for all of humanity, including nature, despite what seems to be occurring around us. We can move forward fortuitously.

Where can we make room for ourselves to be still, to grow, mature, and strengthen our roots in unity consciousness?

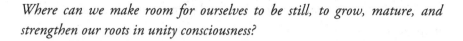

What nutrients and/or symbiotic partners may we welcome to nourish our roots?

How may we rectify any form of weed or decay in our internal systems of thinking, feeling and acting?

How can we support ecosystem regeneration by offering others a branch or two?

Mindfulness practices allow these transitions to occur within our change management models. They call for awareness of the shifts that need to occur and how we may do so by grieving what has been to successfully leap forward into the new quantum realities that are needed.

The dignity® approach is one framework for viewing the mindset and behavioural shifts we need to rebalance predominant divine masculine energy with feminine qualities of gratitude and nurturance. As we conduct our due diligence by percolating the intelligence from our institutional knowledge and that of generative AI systems, we will seek to bolster the mature divine masculine energy of calm, contemplative flow needed more today than our contemporary rush-hour, short-term thinking. Unfortunately, so much of how we operate is anxiety-ridden and reactive for now. This can transition to a response state where we are not shocked by 'disruptions' because we are firmly rooted in how we operate, why we operate and how we will keep operating. This can happen with prudence, consciousness and community. It first begins with us as leaders and managers.

To reach here, we will need to remember *our natural state.*

The future of our communities is infinite and exciting as we start returning to our whole selves more and more. We each have an identity to come home to, embrace, and heal. And then magic happens. We attract our tribe! This gives us the courage to venture out of our comfort zones because we know we are held and have a place where we belong to co-create the reality we wish to manifest around us that serves the highest good for all. This feeling of belonging has eluded us for centuries as our ancestors got displaced or migrated for 'greener pastures'. This has left us as global nomads with the ease of budget travel and increased connectivity to continue feeling 'displaced' and seeking a place to call home. What we forget is that where we are at is equally important as well. There has been a certain history in which we have built an affinity with space, and it deserves our reverence for all it has offered us – the good and the bad. In exchange, we can remember that we have always belonged to ourselves regardless of the stories and emotional baggage we have inherited that make us think otherwise.

In harnessing interdependent communities, we must understand and respect boundaries. We neither seek to heal others nor be healed by others because we are self-healing. We do not interfere or seek attention. We are inwardly focused on outwardly influencing the people and circumstances we are in to shift it to higher vibrational possibilities. In doing so, we will not feel drained or exploited because we always uphold dignity consciousness. We do not take on another's burdens, and we do not judge. We empathise as we can understand our universal struggles and show others how to overcome what they might think is impossible. We do this without needing to offer unsolicited advice. We are waiting to respond instead by holding space.

Partnerships in this realm are co-beneficial because the power play between actors does not exist. Both parties are co-creating new values that can further extend the impact of their work. The interdependence of resources is well-managed, keeping the actors' dignity intact.

Interdependence is, therefore, a constant state of authentic renewal for community-building with reciprocity to ensure everyone is included and shares ownership. We follow through on what we can offer or accept with authentic disclosures. False hope does not exist because we openly communicate what our intentions are and make realistic adjustments in order to achieve a more likely outcome. Trust emerges instead and supports us in knowing we are not alone. This sense of solidarity requires partners to show up as they are without smoke and mirrors.

However, the ideological differences within a community can also make us go against one another. And this is where we can know and internalise that nothing is personal. The politics, the pain of being separate, and ignorance are part of our process of returning to ourselves and each other. The more we realise we are in this together at different stages of our evolution, the quicker we can forgive and let resentments go. We are less likely to force ourselves to fit into places as well. We need to accept that naturally, we will ruffle each other's feathers at some point because we are helping one another grow in our awareness of our behaviours, thoughts and actions.

Ascending our consciousness helps us reach these elevated states of knowing. With constant purification of our thoughts, emotions, and actions, we eventually reach a quiet mind, healed emotions, and values-aligned action. We can return non-love with love and be confident in the trajectories we embark on, knowing there is no one way and that we will be guided as we proceed. We only know this when we venture out. With adequate community support, this self-discovery journey can be tremendously useful. Just the sheer fact of knowing we have someone or something to fall back on makes a big difference.

Every day, we engage and associate with different individuals or stakeholders. We can better manage these interpersonal risks by learning to differentiate between our conditioning, others' projections, and performance expectations. In each moment, we can choose to show up better for ourselves by connecting with another, being fully present and letting go of judgments, especially of ourselves. If we have nothing to contribute to a conversation, we still contribute by listening. If we are not heard, we can ask for an opportunity to share. There is room for our needs to be met. We need courage to be healed, to refrain from our unhealthy habits and to regulate ourselves to a balanced state of well-being.

And communities that allow this space for everyone to improvise and be themselves in each moment thrive the most. Like Nature, we allow the diversity of our beinghood to co-exist when it might otherwise not have made sense.

Out of this 'chaos' usually comes a beautiful synchronicity of understanding, which is organic and ground-up, assuring ownership by all to take care of what they have built together.

Governance in these communities transcends the need for order and moves into mutualism and symbiotic relationships to meet our needs. We are free. This happens when we heal our 'fear of others' or any fear. We let go of our agendas and promote ourselves from a dignified space of asking and sharing what we need without dependence, lack or judgment. Until then, we can keep observing, correcting our behaviours and reflecting on our dignity consciousness. As for our environments, we can observe, flag or speak up about it and extract ourselves if needed because we are responsible. We know how to keep ourselves safe and believe there is always space for us in this big universe.

Solidarity in this knowing can create the multiplier effects we need in our society – that we are all self-healing and, therefore, whole. Our external circumstances do not determine our inner wellness. We do. We are always safe. This is where dogma, beliefs and superstitions that invoke fear-based programming can be lovingly healed within us. We are not being punished. Every moment is teachable instead and showcases how much adversity we can overcome. When we start sharing, we can gain deeper insights into the universal experiences most of us think we are encountering alone – when, in fact, we are not.

When we can allow ourselves to communicate honestly, with appropriate disclosure and compassion for ourselves so that we are not putting ourselves out as well, we reach newer levels of unity within and outside of ourselves. We feel less separate and have moments of closure to properly grieve what was not meant to be ours in the first place.

When we deflect these moments of growth with one another out of fear of rejection or fear of judgement, we risk raising false hope and illusions of who we are. We shortchange ourselves by not deepening our relationships with one another. This is more harmful to us than anyone else. When we return home to ourselves, we understand this is self-betrayal because we are not being real. There are two possible outcomes. First, we might eventually allow guilt or shame to overcome us, which we might use to compound our insecurities. This can derail us further and cause us to act out in other ways. Second, if we avoid reflecting on these incidents instead, we will likely abandon ourselves and keep repeating these behaviours until someone we did not wish to hurt gets hurt. Both consequences allow massive healing where we can be patient and kind towards ourselves for being this way. Where and when did this behaviour originate? What is the worst thing that can happen if we share our truths with others? We are allowed to make mistakes, we are allowed to trial and error, and we are allowed to bounce back better. Let us give ourselves and others this grace of understanding and space to rediscover who we are. We can free ourselves from preconceived notions of who we once were and who we need to be. None of that matters except this present-moment version of ourselves where we are being real with ourselves first and foremost.

In communities where we aim for solidarity, we inwardly reflect whenever we encounter something we dislike in another as a reflection on a possible repressed aspect of ourselves. This information appears from our resonance field, where even perceived 'negative' content can show up for our healing. Using each other as mirrors for our self-healing only works at an intuitive level. If we begin to think and process mentally, we will likely get very affected because not everyone's weakness is ours to contend with. As such, be intentional and stay curious instead to see what shows up for us. Since we are all part of a whole, the importance of accepting another as they are means we understand this spiritual principle. We each possess the light and dark aspects, and the more we integrate our shadow, the deeper our understanding of this will be. We can begin to tell ourselves we are no longer in competition with ourselves and, therefore, with another. We are not accepting falsities or raising false hope out of perceived fears or societal culture. We respect and pursue our boundaries as we act on our values, which inevitably helps other individuals to awaken.

We cannot control others or outcomes. We can only focus on growing our levels of consciousness to see beyond what is apparent and co-create a better world where we are responsive, self-loving, and, therefore, safe. We let go of expecting the worst, even where there is a heightened sense of vulnerability towards bad actors. As we work towards freedom from others, freedom from desires and freedom from fear, we accept the dualistic nature of our world and choose light in our every response.

Each time, something challenging happens:

1. Note how we feel and what is coming to the surface to hold ourselves for that moment to go deeper into that feeling – if possible, find a point on our body where we may focus on
2. What does this point feel, look, smell, taste or hear like? Engage all our senses and feel at this point
3. Without overthinking, describe the visions or sensations coming up, and if there is nothing, pose questions to this space – why are you here? What should I know? Try not to imagine, think or visualise

We realise that beyond the fight, flight and freeze reactions, we can respond with what needs to show up to understand why we feel this way. We begin to see ourselves in a new light, which presents the possibility of feeling lighter because we know more about ourselves today than before.

When we keep doing this work, we realise a base emotional imprint has been dormant and triggered. By addressing it, we heal it and realise we are not broken or fragile. If these moments were not so dense and dark sometimes, we could rejoice as this often leads to massive breakthroughs if we keep at it.

When we want something that does not seem to go our way, we can pray for more patience and guidance to show us other ways. In due time, more insights are likely. This is when we can appreciate divine timing—when everything synchronises and aligns to help us meet our highest potential. Our pain, therefore, is our healing balm, as it also contains the solution. This is why we can unlock true power by exercising vulnerability in dignified exchanges with each other.

This time is precious as we make the transits, so may we honour it, honour our healings and honour each other, especially Mother Earth. There is also no time to waste in enjoying each moment of this experience, for what needs to happen is happening, and we can let go. We are part of one consciousness – one great big universal community powered by love and joy regardless of how the world appears. Our inner world is all that matters, and through the power of conscious ascension, we can tend to our gardens with the same nourishment and protection as parents offer to their children. As such, we will heal all sources of constriction energy within us as we expand our consciousness. This constriction energy has kept us stuck in the falsehoods of our imagination and needs to be transmuted for us to focus on growth. Growth is safe, and we usually take many baby steps before a giant leap. Let us remember this the next time we feel called to shift or transform. Even a quantum leap is a small change that, when added up, leads to transformative shifts for us and the collective.

Communities hold incredible healing power, and the time for action is now.

Expanding our consciousness allows us to let go of selfish tendencies that lead us to hoard and disconnect. Instead, we embrace our inherent worth and unite with ourselves, the Earth, and one another. As we cultivate a deep reverence for the life-sustaining forces around us, we humbly accept all that we know and all that remains a mystery. This journey fosters compassion, allowing us to recognise our shared humanity in others. By staying attuned to our higher consciousness, we shield ourselves from the traps of imagination and illusion. Always connected to the source of Truth, we can shine brightly as lighthouses for those around us. Together, we can harness our collective strength to inspire healing and transformation in our communities, and the time is now.

VI

RETHINK NATURE

I n *The Elements of Power: Gadgets, Guns, and the Struggle for a Sustainable Future in the Rare Metal Age,* David S. Abraham invites us to reconsider our relationship with the resources that underpin our modern technology. The book explores the critical role of rare metals, essential for everything from smartphones to military hardware, and the profound impacts their extraction and use have on both the environment and society. Abraham's examination reveals that dependence on these metals often leads to significant environmental degradation, limiting our freedom to enjoy a clean and safe planet. As pollution and resource depletion take their toll, we are reminded that true freedom encompasses individual choices and our collective ability to live in harmony with nature.

Moreover, the book challenges the prevailing economic systems prioritising short-term profits over long-term sustainability. By emphasising the need for ethical sourcing and innovative practices, Abraham argues for a redefined economic freedom that supports resilient communities and prioritises the well-being of people and the planet. Social justice also emerges as a vital theme. Abraham sheds light on how marginalised communities often bear the brunt of environmental harm caused by resource extraction. This reality underscores the need to advocate for responsible management of our resources, ensuring that all voices are heard and that every community has the freedom to thrive.

At the heart of Abraham's message is the importance of awareness. By encouraging us to reflect on our technological choices' environmental and societal consequences, he empowers us as consumers and citizens to reclaim our agency. This newfound awareness can lead to informed decisions that align with sustainable values, fostering a future where our freedoms are preserved and enhanced. Finally, the book prompts us to rethink our relationship with technology itself. As we navigate an increasingly complex landscape, it is crucial to prioritise innovations that embrace sustainability. By doing so, we ensure that future generations inherit a world rich in possibilities, where they can enjoy the freedom to thrive in a balanced and healthy ecosystem. In essence, *The Elements of Power* is a powerful reminder that our choices today have lasting implications for our freedoms tomorrow. By embracing sustainability as a core value, we can forge a more just and equitable future where people and the planet can flourish together.

Metaphysics is not just about material commodities; it also *involves addressing and restoring a complex natural balance.*

Once we take an ecosystem services approach, we can see how our unconscious decisions of today can affect our availability for choice of natural resources in the near to medium term. Globally, food security is a pressing issue. With our agricultural and food production systems dependent on interdependent factors ranging from good weather conditions to soil fertility to clean water availability, the trade-offs of how we manage our systems from continued environmental degradation cannot continue to be overlooked. Even our consumer habits must change to encourage positive market demand for more sustainably sourced products with smaller carbon footprints supporting local farmers and livelihoods.

We stand at a pivotal moment where new ideas and ways of thinking can spark the creation of jobs that sustain and regenerate our precious resources. Imagine a world where every resource is used carefully, honouring all beings while ensuring a lasting supply for future generations. Now is the time to embrace a holistic and respectful approach to what truly matters. As we tackle climate change with a focus on decarbonisation, let's envision a broader horizon that includes water conservation and the protection of our ecosystems. By doing so, we can ensure that as we advance technologically, we preserve our choices and our planet's health.

Rethinking nature requires us to reflect on our relationship with Nature and how we became disconnected from it. Nature and community are helmed by centennial trees and elders who hold space for younger generations to go through the rites of passage they need to get where they must be. With these changing times, we need more of us to step up as elders to guide the younger generations coming in to step into their true selves and contribute to the evolution of this planet through innovative circular design or nature-based solutions for the restoration and regeneration of our ecosystems. These elders are both knowledgeable and self-aware to ensure the integrity of our communities is resilient in the face of any change and that we can stand together united. For this to occur, our divine feminine needs the strong support of our sacred masculine, which creates a safe space for sustainable emergence to happen within us.

As I write this, I contemplate my journey towards Sustainability Inside-Out™ and how much more I want to achieve. Self-sufficiency and self-mastery are within reach when we can clear the 'noise' in our heads. As a proactive investigator and observer, I have done many experiments and gathered much intelligence on how things are done. I have understood we need a particular resonance for more people to understand what Sustainability Inside-Out™ means. Resonance helps us connect with what is happening or being said around us. It is the field where if our doctor tells us something is harmful to our health, such as smoking, we will give it up because we are in the resonance field of love and self-love. However, when we are not in resonance or when our true resonance is disrupted by 'noise' from external environments or our mind, we cannot resonate. We need to tune up again to resonate and receive; we need a heightened awareness of what is happening within us. I am slowly understanding this process now as I witness it within myself. It requires a form of trust that is grounded in self-knowledge and self-confidence.

It requires us to love ourselves so that we do not wish to hurt ourselves any more.

We all need to be recognised, which is why our divine masculine works so hard. Depending on what we are here to learn, the outcomes of our efforts manifest differently. We traditionally gain self-confidence when we are loved and supported by our family. We conventionally feel respected when we can expect equal rights through our legal systems. And often, it is our career achievements that boost our self-esteem.[37]

How may we balance this, especially if we come from dysfunctional homes, corrupted systems, and unpredictable appraisal schemes? We can go inward: We can be transparent ourselves, learn to self-soothe when difficult situations occur, and learn to reward ourselves with new skills, hobbies, and roles that make us feel equally, if not more, fulfilled.

Rethinking our internal nature will help harness a more robust worldview. We will be able to nurture the exact environments needed to support future generations coming in to seed remarkable innovations and gifts for the New Earth. Table 10 below shows the variance of 'trust' with its extreme possibilities of 1) blind faith when we over-trust and 2) hypervigilance when we cannot trust. It highlights the benefits of balancing to achieve trust within ourselves and around us. Globally, when crises arise, we focus on symptoms instead of signs and are primarily reactive instead of preventive. While it is challenging to make system-wide changes to more sustainable practices, it does require an acute awareness of what is and is not beneficial for us from a well-being point of view. On the environmental level, our intrinsic physiology of anger is being externalised in ways we take ourselves and Nature for granted. As a result, many of us have been and continue to be merely subsisting when we could be thriving. How can we create more trust so that we can start addressing our underlying pain and heal our relationships with each other and Mother Earth?

---

[37]   C.C. Gould, (2008). Recognition in Redistribution: Care and Diversity in Global Justice. *The Southern Journal of Philosophy Vol. XLVI*, p.98, http://www. carolcgould.com/uploads/1/2/5/0/12505497/published_article_recognition_ in_redistribution.pdf

HUMAN NATURE

	← Blind Faith	Trust	Hypervigilance →
BELIEFS	• Challenge: Feel exposed	• Challenge: Unable to explain how we are being guided	• Challenge: Feel judged
	• Fear of authority	• No fear	• Fear of others
	• Give power away to something or someone	• Self-sovereign	• Entitled: people owe me
	• Hopeful	• Self-mastery within the limits/constraints	• Negative thinking leading to more fear
	• Restriction energy: i.e. we cannot do this, we cannot do that	• Freedom energy: Where can I let go and surrender more?	• Constriction energy: i.e. who is out to get me?
	• Wounded divine feminine energy	• Balanced feminine and masculine energy	• Wounded divine masculine energy

Table 10: The benefits of being able to trust

What is our connection with our breath? Our internal regulator system sends us signals when our nervous system is in overdrive.

What is our connection with water? Our paternal linkage to safety? It is a fact that we cannot survive without water. What are we doing to honour it, constantly hydrate ourselves and protect it?

What is our connection with the environment, Mother Earth? Our maternal linkage to nourishment?

How may we heal our emotional and mental blockages to reconnect with the environment?

We all want to feel safe and secure – what does that look like?

We all want to be cared for and extend care to others – what does that look like?

It is evident that we have embraced certain conveniences in life due to the stressors and demands of our fast-paced, globalised markets, where different stock exchanges operate around the clock—hence the saying, "the market never sleeps." In these areas, the space for connection and meaning-making is superseded by a drive to make a difference in the capital markets, dividend payouts, and bonuses. When we consider our relationship with Mother Earth, how we treat her reflects how we treat ourselves. Therefore, we need to rethink our approach to Nature with care. Is our rapid development wise in terms of using finite natural resources? How can we promote blended finance instruments for investments in early-stage research and development of new green energy and clean technologies? How can we adapt our current consumption patterns, review our habits, and adopt more conscious practices? Moreover, when will we start taking responsibility for ourselves and the planet?

Like most of our extraction, production and procurement processes, we need to

- *redesign* our lives to be more purpose-fit (only take what we need),
- *reduce* what we can (by only using what we need),
- *recycle* consistently (to avoid contamination and filling landfills),
- *reuse* what is in proper condition (to avoid the landfill)

These dependencies will be challenged if we continue to take our urban lifestyles and access to convenient purchases for granted. As consumers, we hold much power in defining the responsible sourcing of upstream material, usually extracted from Nature. We must inspire others to learn more and make changes where possible. Despite the growth of eco-labels and third-party verification schemes, we can still be misled if we judge a product by its cover. Reading the manufacturing details and ingredient lists to ensure a product is sustainably sourced will help us make more informed decisions. We also benefit from adopting a more natural lifestyle, on the whole, by using products that do not pollute our waste streams with harmful chemicals. These plant-based products also tend to be free from air pollutants and skin irritants.

Globally, the return to Nature has begun with more movements promoting plant medicine, nutritious recipes, homegrown ingredients and communal gatherings to respect our lunar cycles and seasonal changes. As beings of nature, composed of at least 70 per cent water, we flourish in such natural and flowing states. By embracing this transformative power Nature offers us, we can reconnect with ourselves and one another. However, returning to Mother Earth is more challenging if we have 'imbalances' such as limited bandwidth, short-term thinking, groupthink, and a scarcity mindset instead of an abundant one. We all want stability, a sense of certainty that might seem elusive now. We are quantum beings, and by understanding both spiritual laws and the quantum field, we can take procedural steps towards our true happiness of meeting all of ourselves. Mindfulness helps us unpack what lies in our path towards our true destiny and heal from deep within us. It is often not what our social conditioning or cultures of our current time show or tell us what we 'want'. These visions for our bliss come from within us and will likely look different for each of us.

Our ego is *the* barrier to loving ourselves fully and unconditionally. The intolerant aspect of our being is equally indifferent to our misery from striving to keep up with it.

Following our *dharma* is our true nature, and deep down, we know this. If our dharma is to help others, we must be mindful not to overextend ourselves by taking on another's burdens. This often manifests as a caregiver burden and can also affect non-caregivers through a bystander effect. This is where focusing on expanding our consciousness helps. It brings to our attention much-needed remedies to our everyday issues. When we realise we have taken on another's burdens, we can recognise it is not ours to have, and we need not feel guilty. We each have our trials and tribulations in life. For instance, people who make us feel bad for having a 'good' life often have a wounded divine feminine energy, and we can forgive them and hold space for them instead. Simultaneously, we can reflect on how we might be sharing the goodness in our lives in ways that uplift and empower others to lead the same.

This awareness saves us much misery and ensures we can hone our energies to live in this moment and accomplish what we need for our growth journeys and those of others. We are interdependent when we can fulfil our needs to meet one another on the same page and level up. Expecting or depending on another is what we have come to Earth to heal and overcome. It is generational inheritance at its best as we have had to grapple with patriarchal systems and resistance movements that have had a profound effect of 'separation' or 'not feeling included' imprinted in our DNA. When we are in a zero-state mind and trauma-free, we activate and hone our creativity to bring forth solutions we did not know existed before. We lead lovingly, with little to no desperation, knowing no drastic action is required for goodness and love to come into our lives. Instead, we make gradual shifts and take quantum leaps to transform how we think and act so that we always feel safe and loved.

We are all essentially on a path towards joy and transformation. True joy comes when we know the value of pain in contrast. Transformation comes when we can change the state of something to something better. A healing crisis does that for each one of us. It breaks us down when we realise at another awakened level that we have been scared this whole time and, therefore, making excuses for not moving forward. We have been in our way by blocking our pathway or thinking we are not enough.

I know this well because, despite my best attempts to grow spiritually, I have attempted to bypass some of the tougher emotions and energetic blockages within me simply by using affirmations or auto-suggestions as they are known these days. I tell myself I am healed of this, and I move on. However, that is not how the transformation can unfold. Figure 15 below clearly shows that building trust within ourselves is neither linear nor straightforward. It is a constant unfolding of different layers of discovery for us to meet ourselves authentically and heal what we can now.

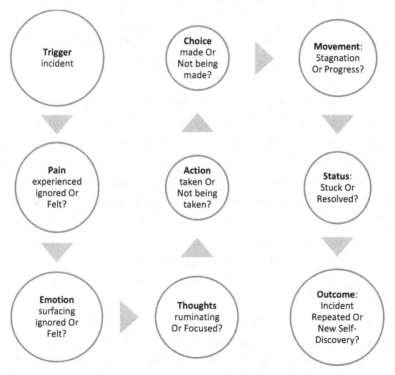

Figure 15: Understanding that healing has a method to its madness can be reassuring

The many layers to our hurt impact us more than we know. As mentioned above, how we treat ourselves is how we treat others and, eventually, if we even think about Nature, how we consider and respect natural resources or our planet. This is, therefore, an opportunity to reflect and grow whenever we argue with someone we love or work with. Often, each party does not intend to hurt the other; we avoid saying what we need either because we are unaware of it until further reflection or we are distracted by a trigger from the argument. If there is remorse after, depending on our ego – we might apologise or not, causing further misunderstandings or hurt. Triggers are interesting. They are often not associated with the person we might be arguing with in the first place. It usually comes from a deep-seated space of injustice or wrong-doing from a long-forgotten memory or unknown time. But it always comes up to be addressed respectfully and healed. However, we might use our ego as a defence instead and miss this opportunity to heal. We might brush these trigger events aside by casting blame towards another person instead.

The question then emerges – how may we accept different views when our ego is in the way?

The ego is competition with ourselves – how we need to keep levelling up. It might be fun at first, especially when we hit a home run or several successes in a row, albeit it often comes with a few failures as stepping stones. Like using Photoshop, we tend to blur out the details of failure stories because we want to look invincible, and that is fine until we start getting worn out and dried out from the constant push towards 'always looking so good' or 'success' in general. We forget the initial moments of joy we encountered from overcoming a hurdle and achieving our first milestone—this sense of adventure, self-discovery of our limits and what we can do. When we raise our awareness, we notice the nuances and begin requiring a reset.

So, how can we support ourselves and one another through ego-deaths and the shedding of older and more uncomfortable layers of ourselves that no longer serve us? We may begin by helping ourselves and others avoid criticising and judging, as well as shame and embarrassment, as our initial feelings. This would help prevent us from falling further into the abysses created by healing discovery. Nature constantly evolves with devasting destruction if we consider the raging and spontaneous wildfires that strip acres of forest and different species. It also resurrects with new plant growth and repopulation, although it mostly requires human intervention, given how much we have lost. We are one of the species in Nature, which is also coded in our DNA. We can adapt, and we can grow; we can bounce back. We need to start remembering that.

Hence, we must respect our humanity by recognising and soothing our pain with kind words and encouragement. Nature does not expect or forecast its losses and gains. Nature is, and our humanity is made up to be multi-faceted and complicated. We stand to benefit more from understanding, embracing all its 'good' and 'messy' aspects to begin putting ourselves back together, although we were never broken. We simply inherited missing pieces of our puzzle from unresolved trauma patterns, intergenerational survival tactics and current live suffering. And when we have our whole self integrated and put together, the magic of our true potential begins.

But how does this happen? How do we let what we need to do come to the surface?

It begins with many levels of purification work on the physical and subtle bodies, especially our thoughts and emotions (as shown in Figure 15). We are not as brittle as this process might make us feel. Each time we walk through the process and come to the point of realisation, we are likely to be met with grief. The grief of how did I not know better? How could I have done this to myself or another? As we process it and feel it, we naturally surrender because we reach a point of no return regarding our humanity. Like Nature, we are not in control here. While we do attract, create and manifest outcomes into our lives, we need to be consciously aware at all times to say we have some level of control, but even the outcomes, especially about when it will happen and if something will happen, largely out of our hands specifically in highly complex multi-variable scenarios.

Being grounded through these realisations and where we intend to head will help us reach clear intentions. Along the way, noticing the challenges and roadblocks on our path will help us narrow down the specifics further. Yes, we are limitless and can do anything we wish; however, most of us are on Earth with precise missions. Further, given planet Earth operates on a linear and chronological timescale, we need to go through our processes to reach the realisations we need to keep building the New World businesses or outlooks.

When we do not feel the pain, we abandon ourselves and often take self-harming actions. This comes in many convenient forms these days. We numb the pain or hide it away until our mind starts to ruminate and remind us about the situation. At this juncture, we might claim we have a headache or lash out at something/someone. This is when our ego holds us back because it begins to feel confronted by its needs and constant push for gratification. It does not want to be weak or vulnerable. We may proceed with life feeling disconnected or more dualistic than usual, knowing what we are showing up with is persona A, but we feel like someone else within.

When we undergo this process of transfiguration, it is a highly inward journey, and we need to respect it. Nature goes through autumn and winter seasons for this exact process of wilting, processing what needs to go and letting it go. She willingly begins the decaying process so that eventual rebirth and new growth can occur. She bids farewell to the animals as they take flight to warmer climates or go into hibernation. She withstands the loneliness of this journey because she knows everything always comes to full circle. Like each day, the sun will rise, the sun will set, the moon will rise, and the moon will set. We are the same. Our dark night of the soul is when we discover we have a shadow side to us that needs to be addressed from sheer neglect and to be integrated back into our whole so that we will not be surprised, disgusted or ashamed anymore. It is as much a part of us as it is of Nature. And we are made with this higher consciousness to heal, to be the new ancestor for our future generations.

If you are reading this, we are being called to shed away what our ancestors could not. In doing so, we can restore balance to our family lines and bring our souls more online. Transmuting our pain into lessons for us to learn provides the reframe for us to take on this responsibility with strength.

With increased awareness of its blessing for us to reclaim our power, we become more attuned to this process, and the emotions will not derail us as much as they might have initially. I believe this rational way of thinking can help us all understand this process as more like peeling away what no longer serves us, like how our bodies rejuvenate our skin. As intelligent beings, we want to do this as consciously as possible to save ourselves from the pain of it happening unknowingly because we are still largely unaware. This is happening now as many of us are distracted yet undergoing change and unaware of how to deal with it. If we are kind to ourselves, we might address it with therapy or speak with a trusted friend. If we are unkind to ourselves, we might prefer to avoid, numb or continuously distract ourselves.

What will help in this instance is recognising our relationship with conflict or 'conflicting views' – *is there any fear of addressing it, and where is it coming from? Why do we defend/justify ourselves, and where did this behaviour originate?*

Do we know our needs and dare to ask for them? Or have we fallen into traps of performing our roles as overly receptive beings for power imbalances to continue playing out? Let us note where we tend to ask most questions – what topics are these, and if this is where we perceive our weaknesses to lie? Or has it been habitual for us to ask these questions because it makes us look a certain way or project a particular image – such as playing the devil's advocate to be perceived as intelligent?

How can we, then, bring down such these walls we have constructed within us? How may we reconnect with ourselves when the ego is present?

Where have we been *too* allowing?

Where have we been ...waiting and worrying for things to happen? This is a stalling, let's–wait–and–see energy due to a lack of clarity. How may we move into trust instead?

How do we find our inner compass to guide ourselves instead of turning outward to others, social media, tarot, etc?

We may also explore where we have feared handling situations or responsibility.

Are there sources of information that accurately see our lived realities and offer practicable insights to help us solve problems or make necessary changes?

What can we do to always be present within ourselves?

What do we do to tell ourselves we are eternally safe? Especially in a world that constantly bombards us with fearful messaging.

It is never too late. *How may we connect with others by allowing them into our lives?* How can we appreciate the diversity we hone and make space to keep these differences growing together? How may we release our expectations and include ourselves in loving connections that accept and support us just as we are without having to overgive or be someone else?

Nature has survived on ecosystem-level support from various plants, fungi, insects and animals forming interdependent relationships. Those that do not merely phase out. These natural laws are no different from how we are meant to evolve and co-exist here on Earth. Those of us unwilling or unable to heal will tend to find ourselves lonely and isolated, albeit technology helps with accessing new friends or additional support. However, authentic communal and humane exchanges make us all come to life fully, and we can make this possible for us, one step at a time. The questions above are some thought processes I undertook to gain my epiphanies of the life I would like to live: happy, joyous and full of meaning-making opportunities based on what I am meant to embody to live out my full potential on Earth. It is hard work and has been a constant grind for me. The universe does tell me to slow down and to trust the seasons of my body and lean into these down times because I will need it before I am to surge up and go running again.

Nature holds so much space for us with its changing seasons. For those of us in urbanised and tropical cities, our cultural traditions and festivals can indicate when we may slow down, reconnect with others and celebrate the simple moments in life. Integration is key. What we learn and internalise at the individual level must also translate to our systems level. Everything on Earth is living, including the systems that run our transportation networks, bank security, and law enforcement agencies. Like humans, these systems also need healing, beginning at the consciousness level. The more we awaken to the limitations we have imposed on ourselves, the more we can open up to new information, ways of doing things, and methods of thinking for our systems to heal. The world may appear more chaotic now, but this also signals a significant opportunity for transformation. Addressing complex risks and emerging successfully on the other side is achievable by leveraging each other's strengths and synchronising our efforts to enhance the collective good, not just the individual entities such as communities and organisations we belong to or represent. When we are receptive to what we need to adjust towards to welcome more prosperity into our lives, we potentially embody the Sustainability Inside-Out™ perspective.

This requires timeliness and patience as integrating everything we know and finding balanced solutions takes time. We must use this time to plan and gather all our resources and information before taking the next critical step. Having a higher vision helps us attune ourselves to the required alignment. This allows us to let go of what no longer serves us. Our knee-jerk reactions are based on fleeting fear-based feelings mostly stemming from our unconscious limiting beliefs about what we are capable of. Instead, we can understand our competencies and how we may best contribute without projecting a larger-than-life reality of our abilities, which may result in mismanaged expectations from others and burnout.

This begins with assuming *less* and *clarifying* more.

This requires us to trust ourselves in an era of confusion and doubt about our future outcomes. This is where we may go inward to build our resolve to connect with ourselves in ways we never did before to remain resilient and unshakeable because we know who we are. This includes awareness of our values, *dharma* and multi-dimensional self. It also requires tremendous self-honesty and compassion to look at our flaws and accept them. We can tell ourselves that we did not know better. We would forgive ourselves if we did. We can realise where we have been patronising towards another, where we overlooked their insecurities masked in unexpected behaviours. We can shift towards holding space for them to come to terms with their fragile humanity, too. Recognising a semblance of ourselves in them and helping each other ascend as we go along will help us realise we are not alone. We have each other.

True freedom is also about accepting that while we have free choice to pick, the outcomes of our lived experiences will still primarily be centred around the same heart openings we need to ascend or spiritually evolve. As such, there is no right or wrong choice. This is something that each one of us will eventually see when we join the dots. We hone in on the process by inviting our divine feminine aspect to come more online from within us. This is the aspect of us who knows we can slow down, be one with all and make time for what is necessary to be sustainable. This includes a deep reverence for Mother Earth and all we receive from her. We understand how to nurture our connection by being mindful.

How do we unravel and free ourselves from 'toxic' people and situations? When we heal ourselves of our *separation anxiety* to see the *humanity* of our *'perpetrators'* behind the 'toxic' behaviours and conditions.

Sustainability Inside-Out™ is one framework that offers a layered understanding of why we act or perform the way we do. Many layers bound us: *karmic*, cosmic (what we decided we would learn from each other before reincarnating), relational (bloodlines and family ties), intergenerational (what got skipped in a particular generation to manifest in our lifetime), as well as additional lessons we wish to learn and harness our abilities from. There are additional interferences in the form of empathic, telepathic exchanges that, if we are unaware of can 'manipulate' us as we remain in a trance-like, medium state of receptivity as opposed to if we awaken, awaken to being conscious of what we are transmitting and what others are transmitting to us non-verbally and psychically. Body language is one example of the non-verbal cues we pick up from others, which impacts us whether we know it or not. Figure 16 outlines key types of information relating to our multi-dimensional self-utilised in the Sustainability Inside-Out™ framework. Overcoming these 'interferences' requires a clear mind connected to our inner guidance system or heart space.

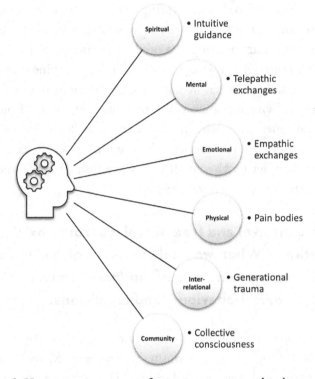

Figure 16: How we can receive information as our multi-dimensional Self

When we step into heart-based leadership, we begin to discern from our heart instead of creating pros and cons lists, seeking reassurances from others or Googling. We are one with our *dharma* because the heart always knows best. This means we feel what resonates and proceed based on the calmness we experience. In this state, no extreme feeling exists – no fear or joy. Instead, an inner stillness helps us to keep moving forward without developing expectations or brewing anticipation. For some of us recovering from trauma, this might be an unknown feeling in the beginning, as we might be used to crises, stress or tense emotions, especially when making decisions. Trusting ourselves may be difficult until we understand what it feels like to move forward from a calm, expanded feeling into the new unknown.

This is the power we unlock when we heal our emotions and bring ourselves back to a balanced state of divine feminine and masculine flow. Our intuition flows more smoothly, and we are content. This is possible if we prioritise our inner well-being as much as our external appearance, signified by the relationships and communities we are a part of. We put out what we get, so let us send out only what is pleasing to receive and what is good for us, such as respecting ourselves so that others respect us, too. We understand and appreciate the diversity we bring to each experience. We know nothing is personal; every moment is a stepping stone for our ascension journey. We recognise our choice to make amends and attune ourselves to receive that which is our highest good. We gain wisdom. We become patient. We let go.

We have to keep being honest with ourselves. Where have we been dominant and controlling? What are we holding on to and why?

Given the histories of our times, most of us are reliving the ancestral imprints of generations past where war, famine, and survival were vital. Despite our apparent prosperity and accessibility to convenience, we may still feel disconnected from ourselves and others, which we continue to numb with everyday distractions, comfort food and irrelevant pursuits or conversations. Finding our way back to ourselves requires a reconciliation with this dynamic that harms us in the long term more than serves us in the short term. We are who we are, and our shadow aspect, which has been deeply embarrassing for many of us, is where rich insights and healing await. It includes our ability to fight for ourselves, take up space, and make it up to ourselves. Every trigger is an opening for us to find the genesis of our disconnect and come back online to our true nature. We can feel and trust again as we expand and open to life. It starts with the first step to loving unconditionally – flaws and all.

Many of us struggle with power dynamics. One example is the struggle for dominance and control in interpersonal relationships as per expectations of our gendered roles. We may engage in competition and aggression if our divine masculine is over-active. This may further perpetuate our insecurities because we unconsciously assert ourselves over others as compensation for what we lack. We may also exhibit unhelpful behaviours driven by a need to appear strong or superior. This can lead to manipulative tendencies or the inability to celebrate others' successes, which can be isolating. These imbalances are also disconcerting when we lose a sense of dignity consciousness in overgiving and minimal receiving. We can change this.

We can begin by witnessing our humanity as it is – that we are inherently scared of losing something we have either been taught to be or internalised to fit in. This is not our true self; we can shapeshift for the better. We must because we are deserving of so much love and unconditional support for the beautiful soul that we are. Our societies and resultant socialisation have evolved for the reasons they have to survive over time. As Nature beings, we can thrive by adapting and building our ecosystems. This means letting go of our defences and becoming emotionally present in life. We may reflect a tendency to reject vulnerability and intimacy, often driven by fear, competition, and a reliance on rationality over emotional intelligence. We may do this by suppressing our emotions and over-emphasising our achievements, leading to strained relationships and a lack of authentic connection with ourselves and others. Eventually, we might feel unsafe to be ourselves and believe we must protect ourselves from others and their agendas. We wall up, defend ourselves with rigid boundaries, and isolate ourselves further.

What needs to be done is self-evident *if* we are open to it.

The New World requires us to keep our kindness towards each other by realising that the many layers of our pain do not start with us. It began with our ancestors, our birth, our childhood and the caregiving we received. We often repeat unhealthy patterns of power dynamics learned from before to uncover the lessons we need to heal on Earth. This frequently involves heartaches, grief, and loss until we choose ourselves and go inward. Until we do, we miss seeing ourselves in others as they share, displace, or project their pain. Similarly, we unconsciously keep ourselves stuck in cycles of pain without questioning the patterns from these experiences.

When we acknowledge our humanity – we allow ourselves to feel uncomfortable and disappointed, but not for long. We are equally able to see the other person's humanity and what drives their motives, and we make space for both realities to coexist in harmony. We take measures to be responsible for our happiness while holding space and pausing in our relationships or interactions. As soon as we are aware, we communicate compassionately and transparently to others about our needs to experience less perceived 'hurt' from such situations. So, let us value our triggers and the pain they help us uncover. It shows us what is important and how we may unpack our underlying pain to liberate ourselves from false beliefs. In this instance, we can learn from Nature. There are no pretences and simply raw life force energy. Where there is too much force, rocks get shaped and ridges formed. Where there is softness, we paint landscapes. There is an inherent beauty in all of Nature, even when it withers.

Noticing where we sabotage our happiness and self-growth in the arena of joy and authentic expression is beneficial. It is necessary to practice curiosity as to why we do this. We can then heal this dynamic by assuring ourselves of how safe we are or can make ourselves feel even when we step into the unknown. This means knowing what foundations we require to feel secure and what safeguards we have in place, like harnesses in extreme sports, to take that leap of faith again and again. Most times, a change does not usually take place drastically. It is several baby steps in the making.

How we cope and self-soothe in this process is what we can reflect on – *do we have healthy support systems that support our evolution? People who build us up, co-workers who empathise and family who give us space to grow?*

To whom may we reach out to learn more about healing?

How can we assure ourselves we are free from others and achieve harmony despite what may have happened in the past?

Where can we strike a balance by freeing ourselves of our desires?

Are we willing to understand fear as an energy charge that can help us unlock unity consciousness? How can we reframe our biggest fear now?

We must also investigate how we treat ourselves at our worst. *Why do our identities as so-and-so matter more than our well-being?*

Why do we burn out when we treat others' opinions more than ours?

It is the final quarter of 2024, and I am attending a conference where the panellists are struggling to address the issue of reducing their frequent flying as they discuss sustainable practices. One panellist suggests we could use hologram technology. This would allow speakers to participate without travelling to different countries. It sounds promising until he caveats that this technology remains quite expensive as of now. The panel went on to answer other questions, but I reflected on how we may foster a more harmonious relationship with Nature, even amidst busy travel schedules.

First, we need to consider managing our personal carbon footprint. One effective way to do this is by investing in local projects that create jobs and support ecosystem conservation or restoration. An online search can reveal various opportunities, including eco-tour vendors and conservation-focused non-profits. Engaging with these initiatives in person can amplify our impact and ensure our contributions are used effectively.

As we prepare for our travels, reflecting on our packing choices matters: Do we need to bring everything? Can we incorporate plant-based or greywater-friendly products? How much weight do we intend to pack, and are there ways to downsize further? When considering accommodations, selecting lodgings with energy-efficient controls can make a difference. Regarding local transportation, exploring shared rides with others or eco-friendly options like motorbike travel will also help reduce carbon emissions.

Next, we must embrace responsible and safe consumption where we can. Thanks to the rise of eco-tourism and sustainable hospitality practices, many accommodations are adopting higher standards for food waste management and sustainable building. We are moving toward more conscious consumption, opting for glass bottles instead of plastic. These choices help mitigate the negative environmental and social impacts on the communities we visit. As consumers, we hold significant power in our purchasing decisions. It is important to avoid local vendors or service providers blatantly disregarding their environmental responsibilities, even if their services appear cheaper. Instead, we could encourage them to adopt more environmentally friendly approaches to attract responsible tourists.

Lastly, we need to re-evaluate our learned behaviours. Successful individuals often experience guilt and feel compelled to "give back," but this can lead to counterproductive interactions with local communities. Over-sharing personal information or overpaying for services out of sympathy can inadvertently foster entitlement and dependency, which are ultimately detrimental. Understanding that our success does not create an obligation to others is crucial. Instead of succumbing to guilt, we could understand how to promote fair wages and sustainable business practices to make more reliable income streams for local communities. By recognising how well-intentioned actions can sometimes patronise others, we can restore balance in our relationships and create a more equitable environment for everyone involved.

CONCLUSION:
TIME FOR NEW STORIES

Time in the quantum field is both flexible and malleable. Many are using this knowledge to heal ancestral or karmic patterns from the past while living in the present moment. It can feel like it takes time to manifest new possibilities here on Earth, and we need to stay patient and focus on the process rather than the results. What we wish to achieve will still be necessary; otherwise, we will steer our efforts in an unknown direction. Table 11 offers inspiration for the aspired states in our ascension journeys. As we purify our energetic systems, we welcome more light, illuminating our true nature.

True Abundance	
From...	**To...**
Information	*Intuition*
Imagination	*Manifestation*
Perfection	*Acceptance*
Expectation	*Surrendering*
Doing	*Being*
Controlling	*Trusting*
Restricted	*Free*
Material-only	*Spiritual-material*
Dull	*Magnetic*

Table 11: How we realise our limitless potential

A clear vision, taking the proper action in line with spiritual laws, and surrendering the outcomes of these actions will help us flow with the universe's plan or divine will. While laws, arbitration and systems of operations across society still have to go on, the call to action here is to take a more surrendered approach towards letting go of what we cannot control. Let us choose where to decentralise, delegate, consult, and engage others. Let us stay open to new ideas and possibilities where we may not know what to do. Where we may be stuck, let us work on shifting our internal blockages out first to make space for new ones. Where we may be saying the same thing, let us have the courage to heal outdated beliefs and thinking patterns.

Fear of living is a real challenge for most of us, even in developed countries.

It is the dilemma of avoidance, and we must embrace this shadow to begin opening up to life. Otherwise, we become victims of circumstances or systems. We may fear losing this sense of comfort we have built over time or more recently when we read about turmoil and discomfort in other societies. We may fear change because it might uproot us from this sense of security. We indulge a bit more in settling into this space so that it is harder to move out of it, not knowing it keeps us locked in from within, unable to take certain risks and see other possibilities. On the other hand, living simply, with sufficient capacity to make us feel safe and secure, allows flexibility and makes us more open to spontaneously experiencing new life possibilities. This agility cannot be understated. We are not bogged down by what we think we need to be; instead, we start living according to how we feel, especially concerning others.

I write this book at the crossroads again, this time within myself. A navigation field pops up, and I am looking at signages that read 'enough and worthy' versus 'continuous improvements needed', and I pick – 'enough and worthy'. There is so much to unpack in our universe – so many shadows and the layers to healing will inevitably end someday. We are self-healing, and with this, I walk forward with the recognition that who I have been, who I am and who I am becoming may be different people, and that is ok. That is where the magic of life exists – in the gaps between our identity and deep desires. As I evaluate my options to move forward – what my needs are and what will take me further in my journey- I choose healing.

We are all limitless. Our only core challenge is believing that we are. Belief, as we know, is intangible. It is a felt resonance that everything will always work out as needed. When we believe we are protected, supported, and challenged to keep reaching our highest potential, we allow the universe to co-create with us. However, most of us are still angry that we got separated and abandoned to fend for ourselves. This is further compounded by the fear-based projections of others imposed on us, which keep us feeling more stuck, rigid, and mostly unhappy. True freedom is realising and accepting that we are not as powerless as we think. Indeed, our destiny is unique and largely unknown to us until we align with it and begin experiencing synchronicities. From once living disconnected, we will gradually embrace all definitions of abundance, as shown in Table 11, to realise our specific purpose on Earth. For this to manifest, we must let go of all stories and make room for new ones.

In the New World, we must build trust by accepting what we are intolerant about. We all have our worldviews and preconceptions about life and the world. Many seek answers and may stray according to how vulnerable they are. Trust requires that we do not exploit another in any way. It is a transparent relationship built on awareness of what is appropriate and inappropriate behaviour. For co-prosperity to thrive, we must accept and make amends for how we violate our boundaries and those of others regularly and consistently. We accept marketing ads and campaigns that have made their way into our laptops and mobile phones without realising the subliminal messaging we internalise, even if we are not actively listening or watching the ad. Our subconscious is always listening.

The most considerable corruption of our time is allowing ourselves to be manipulated and pulled away from connecting with our Higher Self, who needs us to be in high vibration and light consciousness even when processing our dark nights of the soul.

Good news: with self-love as our core intention, we can illuminate when we are betraying ourselves and others from achieving union with our higher consciousness.

Trust builds instantaneously if we walk the way of integrity to reinstate beauty in this world with everything we say, think and do. We neither take from someone else nor ourselves; we flourish knowing there is plenty for all, and we can empower ourselves to reach this state of being. To embody this, we must first understand that beauty is in the everyday mundane and equally in death. It is an undying quality of appreciation for all there is and will be. The aesthetic beauty that ensues such a quality of being is enthusiasm in practice. It is a natural by-product of gratitude and immediately noticeable by those who understand true beauty.

Similarly, trust cannot be understated, overused as marketing gimmicks or loosely in political rhetoric. It needs embodied action, and it begins with us so that we can recognise when it is missing. Again, it is crucial to avoid being self-righteous if we notice discrepancies. We are all dualistic. Choosing to be in our light side means we have integrated our dark side into our consciousness, which understands that we each have the propensity to harm. Still, we choose to transmute that energy to heal ourselves and others through acts of service and unconditional love towards others.

We do not voyeuristically watch or laugh at another's misery or state in a trustworthy world. We do not present painful, challenging narratives through watered-down or over-sensationalised news. We are kind and empathic and work together to restore the trust that ensures we all thrive. In this world, we are for one another as much as we are for ourselves. We might begin with ourselves so that we have our awareness working at its peak levels, noting when and where a distorted energy source might arise to lower our vibration. We are determined to stay consistent despite the temptations, and we remind ourselves that finding the middle ground takes time and lots of healing. Till then, we will hold space and be patient.

Yes, transparent, honest and timely information will be required. We will have no issues sharing in a crisis because we know we can work together on a problem. We do not penalise actors who may be laggards; instead, we work with them to bring assurance to another level of trust.

We move past assurance eventually since there is no need to think/worry in a trustworthy world and no fear. We are assured of the intentions of others who follow through with genuine, kind and thoughtful actions. We show up in alignment with our higher selves and what needs to get done.

There is an acceptance that we do not know everything, which is okay as long as we do what we can now. We need not perform as we are allowed to be ourselves. We do not need to take from someone else because we are self-sufficient. We do not give more of ourselves than needed, knowing our cup has to overflow before we do. This means ensuring we can restore and recharge ourselves through simple, means-based living practices that enrich us holistically.

Trust is, therefore, the glue that will keep us together going forward. As we learn to trust and love ourselves ideally, we learn to accept the 'bad' in situations as 'good' because we know there is always more than meets the eye, and we can suspend our judgements by upholding integrity instead.

So, what are we waiting for? Many of us require peer support; others believe that our fear-based programming within ourselves plays up to keep us 'safe' from trying new ideas, experiences or people. We tend to constrict rather than expand when placed in new situations when those who embrace these situations thrive. We start to wonder why we are not more like them or if they might have had some advantage in life that allows them to pursue this innate sense of self-expression and freedom, and perhaps we are not good enough.

The truth is that we are all made of the same Light aspect that remains hidden in some of us and slightly more switched on in others. We envy this light aspect of those who found the switch within themselves. When we start believing we are interconnected instead, the universe can begin working in our favour, showing us all the inroads to that switch within us so that we can be Light too. However, it is past all the fear-based programming, hidden and repressed aspects of ourselves and judgement of others, which might initially prove too overwhelming and impossible for us to succumb, especially if we 'are too busy'.

Somehow, even if we do not intentionally step in this direction, the universe aligns us with this trajectory. Many of us experience our dark night of the soul in our day-to-day and families without realising why we feel so low and what we can do to shift out of it. Instead, we might numb or distract ourselves, which only lengthens the process. If we knew what was unfolding within us, we would willingly witness its lessons to outgrow our old selves. We are at the crossroads in humanity to raise our consciousness and surpass these previously hidden channels within our psyche. We are indeed well supported to find the answers within ourselves since we are all going through this together, and we can let go of our false safety measures – attachments to things/situations that no longer serve us and those in it, as well as external validation requirements socialised in us from young to feel 'enough'.

As discussed in the chapters before, true wealth is the realisation of bliss consciousness. In this state of being, 'what will be will be', and there is no hurry, stress, worry, or anxiety. It is a state of emptiness and fullness at the same time. I experienced this fleetingly one day as I was walking. I was smiling to myself and detached from the reality of what I was doing and where I was at. There was a serene sense of resolution that if this would be my last moment on Earth, I would die content. It had no urgent calls to make or people to see, no previous wishes and most certainly no self-centred thoughts—just the complete absorption of being in that moment.

I kept smiling throughout this experience as I had only read about it in books written by sages or spiritual science texts. To experience it brought me close to tears, for it felt like this was the moment I was always waiting for – this sense of completion or 'enoughness', which went just as abruptly as it emerged. And I could appreciate that. Life has many seasons of ups and downs, trials and triumphs for us to explore and witness, and these bliss-filled moments will come as we stick to the path to purify the mental and emotional pain that comes from growing out of our old and ignorant selves to becoming more aligned with universal love and our life path.

It is said that we all came here to do one thing, our own thing. If we are not, we will usually be in inner turmoil, different from the external challenges one may face in pursuing one's life goals. This is because even if challenges emerge, the heart-brain coherence brings the person through the experience towards their vision in life. In this state, the individual is aware of difficulties but does not give up.

As souls, we are all happy, loving and peaceful at its source. If we feel this is not us, then it is time we start returning to nature – both our nature and the Nature that surrounds us daily. And this is what this book is about – how we may all connect back with that very essence that can free us from our perceived realities at our current level of awareness. We are all creative beings with infinite imagination – it is when we block or do not accept ourselves fully that this essence is not visible or realised in us. It sits as latent potential waiting to be initiated within us. Some call this aspect the shadow, and others call it creative intelligence. It is this repressed aspect of how we think, see, and act about situations that we forget or keep away from because someone told us to when we were younger. Opening our heart's intelligence will grant us access to this self-mastery if we are to overcome the challenges of this time.

When we remain unaware, we end up contributing to the unhealthy environments we are in, and overall, there is a sense of separateness that heightens, making us more cautious than needed and unsafe. We start behaving like a pitcher plant (critically endangered, by the way) – luring prey thanks to our sweet scent only to entrap and ingest if something comes our way as though this is the only way we can thrive. Those of us who choose not to act this way are still complicit when we allow such occurrences to occur at the workplace or in our institutions, which are meant to uphold integrity and justice. We may adopt unhealthy addiction as a result - shoving experiences of 'unfairness' under the rug as long as it does not occur to us, numb or distract ourselves with gadgets or gossip. We would rather someone else sort out the garbage than us and live at this frequency level, seemingly resigned to life, not knowing there is a natural vibrance accorded to each of us if we choose to be brave.

We pad ourselves up even more, share our beliefs in stories and perceptions of everything happening around us, form groups with people who think like us, and further widen the separation gap with polarising views and actions. We do this to survive, escape our inner pain, and not suffer when we are, in fact, creating more suffering. This was who I used to be, and I can openly share that this is not who we are.

This book is, therefore, a clarion call to the Bravehearts within institutions and family units to reframe, forgive, and let go to create a new society, well-being or inner you. No one can unlock our potential except us; it will require positive psychology, inner work, and embracing our shadow side. Detaching from material aspects of life will help tremendously as this distracts us. Instead, a new profound sense of prosperity needs to emerge – one where we are richly content with the simple things in life, especially in the present moment, and we are determined to help others experience this inner joy. There is often an argument that Maslow's hierarchy of needs deter many in Asia from pursuing these higher spiritual aspects, and I wish to counter that.

I am from a humble background and did most of my healing work from my bedroom while living with the very people with whom I shared a 'pain-filled' past while also attracting perceived unhealthy external situations to transmute, heal and develop my consciousness. For most of my healing journey, I was also a caregiver in my family, and I can relate to the struggle of allocating much-needed time for our inner work. Many times, I was distracted and tired, too. All I can say is that my transformation did not happen overnight. It took seven conscious years and probably many more courageous steps before then to lead me on this path of forgiveness and self-forgiveness so that I can create heaven on Earth within my immediate life.

Throughout this journey, I wondered why I always had to be the 'bigger' person, forgive, compromise, and let uncomfortable incidents like perceived injustices pass. This made me question my self-worth, my values, and my self-expression. It led to an eventual breakdown of my old self as I studied various spiritual texts and wisdom teachings that consistently reminded me to turn the other cheek.

Nothing is more important than our inner state of being because it dictates how we see the world. This led to a profound shift in my perspective. Instead of focusing on the people in my life and assigning them roles, I explored the archetypes within my inner world. These archetypes were shaped by past and present traumas, ancestral imprints, and actions from past lives. (Note: This book does not require a belief in reincarnation and encourages an open mind to understand its central message.)

The *sooner* we all realise that our external world is playing out from what is happening *within* us, the *quicker* we can use them as mirrors to our psyche and *heal* ourselves, *once* and *for all.*

This profound healing clears out the family lines we are in and have created, which benefits the whole in unimaginable ways. We are liberated from many limiting beliefs from our old stories of varying dignity violations. We start believing that our quantum leap has led us to new wormholes to explore new worlds where other possibilities previously denied to us exist without questions.

Besides using our external world as mirrors to self-heal, we can use it to build the exact world we wish to see. Rome was not built in a day, and likewise, having a vision of this, followed by higher values and supportive structures to help us manifest ideas into form, will be crucial. This idealism, enthusiasm, and dynamism will help rebuild our world better, and we need everyone's creative potential for innovation to be switched on.

Many spiritual and mystery school teachings talk about the coming of a new age, where a Golden Age will come again, and we shall all be redeemed. Our current time-space continuum supports this potentiality thanks to the rapid technological growth and human development advancements we are achieving (at least in the developed world). What may hold us back from full throttling forward into unimaginable progress and success for all is multi-fold. First, our ego selves, our identification with matter and form, and not knowing what makes us truly happy from within. When we find our flow, we can materialise unconditional love within and around us. When responding instead of reacting, we show our empowerment by embracing creativity to overcome disorientation caused by chaos.

As such, the time for collective leadership has arrived. This is when we work to build virtues of forgiveness, devotion, and transparency to purify our relationships with others. Instead of conforming, we are being called to be courageous co-creators by developing our intuitive service to the Truth.

There is an illusionary façade of the world being difficult, hopeless and unkind. Many of us have accepted this as our reality and, therefore, surrendered ourselves to what we think is the only outcome possible. When we break this façade, we must confront the belief systems and frailties that limit us in such thinking. Overcoming this ignorance of our former selves comes with great courage to see things as they are. It also requires consistently contemplating and growing towards our best selves.

To facilitate our collective leadership, we must return to Nature – acknowledging our multidimensional Self and cultivating deep reverence for Mother Nature, who sustains us.

The deeper we listen, the deeper we open up to what is real around us. This aspect of co-prosperity will need us to reconnect with the purity of our hearts within ourselves. The purity of our own heart that is independent of external circumstances is what we are aiming for. Nothing and no one can wound us because it is not who we are. We become an embodiment of love and can help others to love. This clarifies that our speech, voice, and silence come from a pure place inside us rather than from shadow or fear.

We are all here on Earth to remember, heal, and love. Co-prosperity thrives when we awaken to this because we know we are all part of one heart. We witness this when wars emerge and how even if we are not in the war-afflicted zone, our heart wants to reach out and do something. We want to touch lives and, if possible, make things right again. Even when we are feeling hopeless, we still care.

Purification will be a process that will take time and mindfulness. It will require tremendous shadow work to deal with being alone initially and subsequently integrating what we have learnt by re-engaging with others. To begin with, we will need to transcend our fear-based programming and notion of vanity that we exist as individuals. We must understand how and why we keep people from ourselves and our hearts. Then, we will transition towards being less emotionally overwhelmed or affected by others. By working through our emotional traumas, blocks and armouring, we can release any deep-seated belief that others can take our freedom from us based on this fear-based programming. We will start truly deeply loving from within.

Self-honesty, self-reflection, and communion will help us see where we are holding ourselves back from others. We may find it in the way we think, so strengthening our heart-brain coherence will be helpful as we step into the New World. Co-prosperity will require heart-based communications, refined beyond the trauma patterns and ancestral imprints we have inherited and built over time.

As we let the world in, our hearts will swell with self-love and love of life. We will no longer fear living, fear not living and fear dying. By letting all in, including the wounds of others, we embrace being part of unity consciousness. We have to disentangle from the 'pain' attached to the suffering of others. These are charges that can be accepted and transmuted. It will require courage and conviction to feel better, be more aligned and provide synchronous growth for everyone around us by honouring and respecting our energetic boundaries.

When we heal how we feel, think, and act, we may start to embody this truth as we see how our environments and the people around us shift. Peace begins to manifest from the inner peace we are developing and projecting. Through self-healing, we start becoming a lotus that emerges from muddy waters to connect with a Universal consciousness that propagates compassion, love, and happiness for all.

Oṃ maṇi padme hūṁ
The Jewel is in the Lotus

Yes, the self-healing process will take us into the unknown within our psyche and leave us feeling low for invariable periods. We need not succumb to these painful memories, repressed emotions or low mental states. As Buddha says, all suffering will end once we start seeing things as they are and past the collective veils of emotional imbalance, unfairness, and disadvantage, to name a few. We realise the gems in these experiences when we choose to heal. In the process, we inevitably start becoming self-assured and determined to reconnect with what is real.

There is a sense of homecoming to something and someone, and we find that space within ourselves. We learn to cultivate this inner sense of pride, joy, and love for ourselves and share it with others because we will start overflowing with these qualities. We find what we constantly seek externally within us.

Many of us want to be recognised, and it begins with recognising our authentic selves and adjusting to the 'right' environments that support this goal. Here, 'right' is not used in a moralistic sense. It simply refers to the frequency that matches yours. There are such environments, and we must believe and have faith in attracting these 'more aligned opportunities and relationships to us.'

There is no value judgment because we are all on our learning journeys here. As such, 'negative', 'toxic' or 'unhealthy' are just imbalance states that need to return to equilibrium, and we can make that happen within what is possible based on our level of consciousness. There need not be a grasping or over-extension for us to fix anything or anyone. Learning to accept and allow situations and people to unfold is equally essential. Once we have sufficiently observed, we may share our insights to gather feedback on what others are feeling to support them in their journey.

Self-healing from an individual to a family to a community level causes positive waves of awakening in our collective consciousness. It clears and cleanses unhelpful and limiting thought forms constantly surrounding us, whether articulated or not. We can overcome them by being consciously conscious, not fearful of them. Once this awareness stabilises, we will innately develop the capacity to appreciate the natural intelligence surrounding us every moment. We recognise that there is life in the flora and fauna, appreciate plant medicine, understand the elements' qualities, and seek to co-exist more harmoniously with the knowledge the elemental forces share with us unconditionally.

The potential for co-existing and harnessing the strengths of our living ecosystems within our manufactured environments has tremendous potential for us to restore planet Earth. Nature-based solutions, green buildings and community gardens are all examples of how we are beginning to synergise. We still have a way to go, and it is promising that solutions can emerge organically from the grassroots level to the policies shaping the future to its highest timeline possible.

This New World requires *trust* and maintaining the trust through *ethical conduct*.

It will require us to return to our roots as beings in nature, here to co-exist, instead of unconsciously relegating ourselves to chronic illnesses, depression and loneliness. We are not separate from one another nor from the cosmos in which we all live, work and play. The sooner we can start acknowledging how our actions affect others within our jurisdiction and across the globe, the quicker our ascension back home. We have to start believing, like the introductory scenes to any children's movie welcoming us to suspend our rationality to embrace a sense of wonderment and positive enchantment in co-manifesting hope wherever we may exist.

In doing so, we empower ourselves and others and become free. This shift requires tremendous investment and a rethink in quantifying actual value when making real-world valuation judgements. Actual value comes from various values, not just what services our businesses can offer to create profits. Financial independence from one another is great if it ends dependency and improves self-reliance. Still, it is detrimental to society if we cannot support one another in times of crisis.

This has given rise to gift economies in the West, where the focus is on bartering our time/skills instead of using money as a denomination of valuation. Albeit small, these efforts are likely creating quantum changes at the macro level, which will only benefit us. For example, someone who is already a caregiver but offers to take time to take care of someone else's children is offering higher actual value. Their efforts are from a limited resource bank, given their existing caregiving status, making their offering an act of selfless service.

Therefore, the New World will require new autonomous and regenerative economic models to support the whole. We will require authentic ways of functioning daily to bring holistic balance to us all. Such change has been underway since the global COVID-19 pandemic kick-started multi-country trends in remote and flexible work schemes.

However, power imbalances and co-dependencies have enabled unhealthy dynamics and systems to function for too long. Co-dependency shortchanges our ability to realise our full potential. It keeps us locked into unhealthy ties that tether us to one another based on perceived power imbalances. At our core, we are all the same; this does not change regardless of who we decide to be in this lifetime. Co-dependency supports groupthink; it supports herd mentality – we go where there is a perceived need instead of doing what we are called to do. We aim to uphold the system until it simply cannot. We may struggle to see the point in what we work for or who we work for because we realise our self-betrayal by denying ourselves the dignity of our values and gifts. Yet, we return to the grind daily from a sense of powerlessness that must be overcome.

Like the lotus flower, we can all rise from murky waters to bring new beauty to this world. Like its multi-petal form, we are multidimensional and hold great promise. As such, it is time for us to step out of our way and go deep into these waters to rise above the surface, reborn with splendour to share with all. Spiritual evolution unlocks our ancient DNA, which promises us we are enough and okay. We will pick ourselves up when we fall. We will keep going forward. Joy ensues when we look back and see how far we have come. The many trials and tribulations were, in fact, the opening of layers to our onion skin. By the time we are done, we are many layers deep into ourselves, and we will feel lighter. This requires our commitment to loving ourselves like never before. How we move into this balanced state depends on our awareness of what is triggering and coming up for us to heal so that we can move into self-sovereignty.

'As above, so below' is an ancient knowledge that heaven is on Earth. All we have to do is remember and recreate it. In this book, we explored the grounding knowledge to understand our role in the cosmos and how we, as consumers of products and services from fellow human beings, can interact better with our natural world—starting with nourishing ourselves mentally, physically, emotionally, spiritually, inter-relationally and communally. We humans are social beings. We are loving beings. There has been a disconnect for too long with our linear production systems and ways of thinking. We must reverse this lifestyle choice of taking and making to closing the loops. How may we reuse, upcycle or reimagine the materials on hand to prolong their lifespan and promote creative alternative use?

Such a lifestyle shift only occurs when we awaken to the benefits of redefining what truly matters and sustains us. This often entails a spiritual awakening that can shake our very being and transform us towards a world previously unimagined. As we purify ourselves and open ourselves up to this possibility, we surrender to the purpose of our existence. We are meant to experience the full spectrum of life. When we limit ourselves in one way or another through resistance/deprivation or over-consumption, our energy remains stuck and constricted. By letting go, we expand and allow creative flow to work through us and encourage new streams of thinking, being and acting to emerge. This will go beyond the labels we once inherited for ourselves. It will require suspending what our ego mind has created and detaching through observing ourselves, observing what our heart truly longs for.

This sense of connection to something more profound is what co-prosperity is about. How may we accept others where they are, with compassion, and how may we imagine our societies transforming towards heart-based intelligence rather than development-centric thinking? What would advancement in these types of societies look like, and why does it matter that we maintain or encourage such a momentum instead? We need not look far. Simply looking at our own lives and how we live, we can see if the constant chase for something (usually material) is helping us to be holistically healthy. As energy beings, part one of the book also shares more about the spiritual science and ancient knowledge emerging in our collective consciousness for us all to thrive. We are well supported with best practices and communities living these lifestyles, yet we may not open ourselves up to these realities for many reasons. Why?

'As above, so below' requires that we all acknowledge that heaven is on Earth and comes with conscious manifestation through our thoughts, actions and words. We must commit to suitable actions when we intend to be compassionate, even when trialled and tested, which will occur on this path. This has to be consistent over time, and then it becomes internalised from a grounded, authentic place because we have concurrently explored our shadow side. When we fail to integrate our shadow self, we only show up one-sided in the world and at the surface level. To purify our essence, we must dig deeper and mine the gold of self-mastery. We are all yin and yang, positive and negative. One cannot live without the other, and magic is involved in finding equilibrium.

'As within, so without' – another ancient knowledge stream that our external environments will naturally evolve as we inwardly purify and transform ourselves. We become more in sync with the universe's flow, and more opportunities to connect with like-minded individuals and projects show up. We are committing to the process of unification within us that connects us to everything else around us, including nature. We understand spiritual laws better and show up better for ourselves, others and the natural world.

Co-prosperity emerges when we remember our true selves and build new structures to promote simplicity, groundedness, evolutionary learning, expanded living and, most importantly, true joy from within or bliss. The inner knowing is that come what may, we will be okay. Everything around us is not labelled or perceived as good or bad; just as it is, we flow like water. We do not cling, and we embody the natural intelligence in all beings to stay interconnected. In this line of thinking, how we operate our world shifts to a more conscious, co-creative and innovative space. Boundaries are released, and we can tap into our limitless potential through dignity consciousness. Respect will be fundamental – knowing we are all of equal worth and Mother Earth sustains us, the scales will be tipped back into balance.

This is why we must begin this journey home *now*.

Part two of the book discussed our environments and how we may build heart-based intelligent societies. At the individual level, it will have to begin with us as consumers, end users, employees, leaders, and shareholders.

'Why' has to be our basis for living now. In a world of fast information, big data, and deep fakes, we are becoming increasingly challenged as consumers to know the best product for our evolution. We may have simply been consuming out of survival, unhealthy habits, or to feel a void. This can be healed. Only then will our external environments stop feeding us the exact products and services causing our illnesses, stressors, and striving. Therefore, we will need to ask clear questions to support our continuous growth. When the signs and information we receive offer valuable inputs or insights to our questions, we know how to follow through. We often give our power away to auto-suggestions or viral content that tells us what to focus on instead of going inward to derive our authentic sense of meaning-making. We may also tend to ask or receive advice from people who have gone before us or are older, not realising that they may have a level of influence over us that we may not realise. How they lived and continue to live is not how we need to. We find meaning in different things, and each generational cohort shows that to be true, from the millennials to Gen Z workers.

We only stop caring when we assume, stop being curious and dismiss feedback. We start carving our worlds based on what our inner world looks like, which needs to be disrupted by seeing things as they are. We often hold on to staying disillusioned because it keeps our pain, sorrow and betrayal at bay. We do not want to feel the pain. We numb it by staying fixated on one reality. When we seek heart-based intelligence, we work through these blockages and re-parent ourselves back to healthy, secure beings who see things just as they are, with all the greys and the black and white. Overcoming fears is courageous. It is possible for all of us, and we must celebrate each time we progress to build positive reward systems for our psyche to keep levelling up. This is how we unleash limitless power for ourselves and ensure we are empowered to be our most authentic expression in this lifetime. It will help us see others in a similar light and with compassion, especially those we may have previously perceived as threats or perpetrators of unfair/unjust systems.

We each play our roles in uncovering our light amidst the darkness.

The beauty is that divine justice operates all around us at any point. What we may seem to lose was not ours to begin with, and what we gain is also not ours. We are merely operating on a timeline to live out our highest potential, overriding all systems of fear, persecution, and defence. We are inherently happy, loving, and peaceful spiritual beings having a human experience on Earth. When unsure of ourselves, old fear programming ingrained in our family lines comes up to be cleared. When we are in union with our higher self or consciousness, there is only clarity and oneness. We are not divided into many directions, and we seamlessly flow to the underlying current of our heart-based intelligence, which guides us along our unique pathway in this lifetime. Doubting our best intentions is an opportunity to explore why we fear failure, where it comes from, and why we fear new opportunities. Doubt is steeped in the fear of the unknown, which stems from our need to know and be in control to feel safe.

And when we face a roadblock on this path of exploration into the unknown, we might feel suppressed or limited. Knowing that no one is out to get us is essential, especially if things do not work out as we want. Acknowledging this is fundamental to stepping out of self-pity and into self-empowerment. We are all co-creating our current realities, and what we wish to happen requires consistent, conscious efforts to manifest baby steps. It does not happen overnight; we must keep holding on to the higher vision of progress. It occurs more naturally and synchronously with the universe when it involves our highest good. Additionally, some fabulous souls have taken on a more significant karmic load than others to help clear the family lines of our communities and societies. This requires more time and is not self-sacrificial as we learn so much more in these spaces to step into our highest power as eventual teachers.

Limitations, like roadblocks, need not disempower us. We are not discouraged by others' thoughts and emotions. We can tell which thoughts are ours and what is of the moment. If we constantly worry about the future, we will not see things as they are. We will continuously project our fears or hopes onto the present moment with myriad expectations, only to be disappointed, especially if it is not what our soul journey or purpose is supposed to be. How, then, may we know how to move forward with clarity? Develop questions that serve the highest good and receive what information emerges from within us.

Staying grounded makes us more likely to return to nature when we focus on remembering our true selves. Co-prosperity is about thriving in our ecosystems through a conscious connection to what sustains us, what drives us from within and where we want to be. It requires profound courage to step out of the boxes we have been placed in and pursue the gifts we have been given. It requires us to suspend our old thinking and step into our lives in new, uncharted waters. It requires deep trust that we are held by a cosmic buoy towards our *dharma* when we seek to purify from within.

By accepting life, we acknowledge that the end is also a beginning. This might read as a paradox if we read it on the surface. It holds a profound truth that can help us surrender to any change process. Have heart. What is ending for us is always making way for something else. We are, therefore, never at a loss, which brings us to the fairness and justice problem. Where one generation has been 'looted', the other will gain. Such rebalancing is the natural divine order, and through reverence for all that sustains us, we can align with our intended way of living instead.

As we rebuild with better, fairer governments, consumers must drive demand for goods and services. They should either benefit us or not harm our future. We seek more joy, harmony, and humane conditions for all, including animals. We will need to understand where our food comes from, how long products can last, and what improvements companies are making to ensure our natural resources are being restored and regenerated as we speak. The power is in the hands of consumers to signal the proper market demand for sustainably sourced products and services. It will send more precise signals to investors and product developers on the need to remanufacture or offer add-on services to increase the green value cycle of their business models.

There is, however, a common mindset that everyone wants something from another. How do we co-prosper? How do we see each other at a soul level? This comes from our origin story – what are we saying about ourselves, what are we saying about another, where may we meet? When may we meet, past all the perceived illusions of what keeps us apart? How can we transmute this fundamental void into authenticity and honesty with each other? Where can we let go of the need to fix or thrive off another? Earth needs to heal; we need to heal. Let's be the new ancestor our ancestors called for.

Thank you for joining me as I integrated the critical lessons from my self-realisation journey. My journey to uncover my limits and pains has helped me show up and hold space for others. I am now my most authentic self. I have firm boundaries. I aim for love, especially self-care. I have developed conscious habits that are purpose-fit for me and gained personal sovereignty. The seeking of Truth has kept me grounded my whole life. I am blessed to know a Higher Power guides us. My faith does fade during spiritual tests, but it helps me face self-doubts. It also helps me create an emotionally safe space to move forward. I have newfound gratitude for the process of grief like never before. This is because the end begins this process of letting go, which gets easier each time – much like decluttering our wardrobes.

We must all build strong faith in the unseen and unknown to know we are guided through it all. This human journey is heroic, and I am glad to travel it with you.

> *Self-reliance is the ability to stay grounded, to know when to act, and to interpret the information that comes to us. It is about being reliable to ourselves and showing we will not jeopardise our well-being with more fear. Likewise, for businesses, self-reliance is about accepting change as a constant. Solutions are available for all issues, and we achieve more results when we work together with others, be it within our companies or between business partners.* - From *The Action Gap: Business Strategies for Co-Prosperity.*

REFERENCE LIST

Abraham, D. S., *The Elements of Power: Gadgets, Guns, and the Struggle for a Sustainable Future in the Rare Metal Age*, New Haven, Yale University Press, 14 January 2016.

Bopaiah M., 'Equity: How to Design Organisations Where Everyone Thrives', Oakland, Berett-Koehler Publishers, 9 August 2021.

Borowski, S., American Association for the Advancement of Science (AAAS), *Quantum mechanics and the consciousness connection*, 16 July 2012, https://www.aaas.org/taxonomy/term/10/quantum-mechanics-and-consciousness-connection (Accessed 31 May 2024).

Campomanes, I.; Dannaoui, N.; Lemoine, J. and Negrea, D., Atlantic Council, *The Path to Prosperity: The 2024 Freedom and Prosperity Indexes*, June 25 2024, https://www.atlanticcouncil.org/in-depth-research-reports/report/the-path-to-prosperity-the-2024-freedom-and-prosperity-indexes/ (Accessed 11 September 2024).

Chopra, D., 'Abundance: The Inner Path to Wealth', United States, Harmony Books, 1 March 2022.

Corera, G. and Wheeler, B., BBC News, *AI could 'supercharge' election disinformation, US tells the BBC*, 15 February 2024, https://www.bbc.com/news/world-68295845 (Accessed 12 September 2024).

Fraser, N. and Honneth, A. *Redistribution or Recognition?: A Philosophical Exchange*, London and New York, Verso, 2003.

Fraser, N. 'From Redistribution to Recognition? Dilemmas of Justice in a 'Post-Socialist' Age', in Anne Phillips (ed.), *Feminism And Politics: Oxford Readings In Feminism* (Oxford, 1998; online edn, Oxford Academic, 31 October 2023), https://doi.org/10.1093/oso/9780198782063.003.0021 (Accessed 10 October 2024).

Gould, C.C. (2008). Recognition in Redistribution: Care and Diversity in Global Justice. *The Southern Journal of Philosophy Vol. XLVI, pp.91-103*, http://www.carolcgould.com/uploads/1/2/5/0/12505497/published_article_recognition_in_redistribution.pdf (Accessed 12 September 2024).

Honneth, A. *The Struggle for Recognition: The Moral Grammar of Social Conflicts*, Great Britain, Polity Press, 1995.

Hudson, M., Psychology Today, *What Actually Is Consciousness, And How Did It Evolve?*, 7 October 2023, https://www.psychologytoday.com/us/blog/finding-purpose/202009/what-actually-is-consciousness-and-how-did-it-evolve (Accessed 6 September 2024).

Kaur, D. 'The Action Gap: Business Strategies for Co-Prosperity', Singapore, Partridge, 2024.

Lacy P., Spindler W., Long J., World Economic Forum, *How Can Businesses Accelerate The Transition To A Circular Economy*, 20 January 2020, https://www.weforum.org/agenda/2020/01/how-can-we-accelerate-the-transition-to-a-circular-economy/.

Mishra, V., UN News, *Algorithms should not control what people see, UN chief says, launching Global Principles for Information Integrity*, 24 June 2024, https://news.un.org/en/story/2024/06/1151376 (Accessed 12 September 2024).

Perkowitz, S., Britannica, *E=mc²', September 9 2024*, https://www.britannica.com/science/E-mc2-equation (Accessed 11 September 2024).

Thompson, S. (2005). Is redistribution a form of recognition? comments on the Fraser–Honneth debate. *Critical Review of International Social and Political Philosophy*, *8*(1), 85–102. https://doi.org/10.1080/1369823042000335876

World Economic Forum, *Global Risks Report 2024*, 10 January 2024, https://www.weforum.org/publications/global-risks-report-2024/ (Accessed 14 June 2024).

World Economic Forum, Whitepaper, *Measuring Stakeholder Capitalism Towards Common Metrics and Consistent Reporting of Sustainable Value Creation*, September 2020, https://www.weforum.org/publications/measuring-stakeholder-capitalism-towards-common-metrics-and-consistent-reporting-of-sustainable-value-creation/ (Accessed 15 June 2024).

Yogapedia, *What is Ra Ma Da Sa Say So Hung?*, 21 December 2023, https://www.yogapedia.com/definition/10604/ra-ma-da-sa-sa-say-so-hung (Accessed 31 May 2024).

ABOUT THE AUTHOR

D illpreit is a trained political scientist, sustainability-certified professional, and author of the Co-Prosperity series. In her second book, *Sustainability Inside-Out*™, she offers practical wisdom on how we may all co-prosper by healing our mental and emotional blocks to creative solutions. Leveraging insights from her personal journey, this book succinctly presents a clear win-win-win for people, planet, and prosperity when we return to Nature.

Printed in the United States
by Baker & Taylor Publisher Services